HEIKE THIEME - YLVA

Imprint

Bibliographic information from the German National Library:
© 2024 Heike Thieme
Publisher: BoD • Books on Demand GmbH, In de Tarpen 42, 22848 Norderstedt
Print: Libri Plureos GmbH, Friedensallee 273, 22763 Hamburg
ISBN: 978-3-7597-9577-9

My father, the moon, my mother, who lives in it.
I became the one that none of them knows.
But that's a good thing !

hi, hello friend! Who knows where you are right now?
I've been very relaxed the last few days, even dreaming of my own mother living inside me, a beautiful blonde woman. She is always the same figure, a former neighbor. I felt like she had been adopted from my family all my life, but she still protects me to this day, warns me about others, explains other people's thoughts and intentions to me. She also shows me the family circumstances in which I grew up and how people have developed. This time she was blonde for once, but the same woman, and protected me again, warning me that if there was someone who was trying to hurt me, then I had a duty not to react in the same aggressive way, as long as our connection remains! I am very proud that many women meet me in dreams and praise me for every behavior I have shown.

I have a question. I have never been in a relationship with a man or a woman or anyone else. So I would like to know what someone thinks of me? Am I perhaps the ego type with a great need for patience, attention and care? Or am I seen as a transcendental magical sister who silently looks you in the eye when she has a wish? And who am I after sex? Could the other person be more interested in getting to know me once these first acts are over? And what about his or my dislikes, the lower tolerance for actions or reactions? Am I not a little too interested in all these topics in the whole world? If I am an open woman, is this man irritated by my jokes, desires and spontaneity, or is that the reason for leaving me from the start?

I think I know. I am the magically calmer type.
That's it for today, have a good time, I'm going to prepare myself mentally for a really new good novel, I've wanted to do that for a long time. The lawyer, as usual, is now doing her part of the deal, and maybe I'll get some peace and quiet to paint again.

Anyone who loves his friends,
does not travel to the desert, does not shit on others,
does not complain as a guest, does not aspire to the highest offices,
does not cheat public money, does laugh at all women,
does insist on the power of the church, does not know what to do,
does not call others by their names, does hobby horsing,
does it with one of his daughters, does not show respect for their mischief,
does not make himself into a special being, does not deserve special status!

I have a Good One !
I have now gotten to know a whole number of women properly.
This means that the loud ones, the fascist feminists, don't make a big fuss about it because, in their stormy ways and for the sake of nature, they have clearly already met the wrong man. Unfortunately, that only makes them more and more disgruntled. No one had a good time with them. I thought about it quietly for a while. Women who are mostly known in the Rhineland as fascist feminists. Haved a messed up upbringing. But all the facts always come to light. Not all of them manage to get their hands on the sluggish, wealthy yes-man as their prince, who is so oppressed that he spirals into depression and powerlessly escapes from it.
Some experience the exact opposite, and the man teaches them the lesson of a lifetime. No one is given everything in life for free. Some people have a good understanding of human nature and say to themselves that this encounter would definitely have an expiration date even after years, and this woman will come back to the point of fact, as if from then on she had to make her own sandwiches and her sex didn't mean a trophy for the living room shelf because she was too happy to think a clever man was a fool who she didn't train. From then on, the scales fall from her eyes and she realizes that she has chosen the absolutely wrong profession because not all the fascist feminists in the social work field uncritically think everything is admirable and then roll out the red carpet for her for the rest of her life. From this moment of her raging jealousy, she must realize that this is destroying her relationship and that she has blinded herself with her greed for recognition, attention, fame and to make it big on the show!

Women who probably flee their messed-up parents' home and go into wealth. They only seem to have found a saviour, but all material things have fallen silent, and they experience how their escape into what they have and all the beautiful children are just an excuse for not having started to confront themselves first. So anyone who flees the parental home into marriage is always alone at some point. Either because the initially inexperienced man distances himself from her to have an affair, or because the woman becomes aware of her merry-go-round and the little children develop into the same superficial, spoiled, vain, cold-hearted creatures from whom she once fled. She experiences, like a neighbor girl similar to her, who for many years asks for refuge from the bad pig family, for protection, for mental health, acceptance, and a bit of love, and a space for an undamaged childhood, that this mother recognizes in the girl herself, who was on the verge of drowning all her life. And she adopts the child and takes it under her skirt for the rest of her life, vowing to keep it under her skirt, because every child needs emotional protection, so much responsibility she has made her life's work, while her own children were unable to share her luxury, their hearts closed, and the mother soon wished them as far away as possible, until they were gone too, out of sight and out of mind!

Perhaps there is a negative meaning behind the stronghold that a fascist feminist with tits and charm is trying to get hold of, married to a husband on the island of dreams, into comfort, that this woman is always very quickly caught up in unexpected loneliness. This life lie trapped there in the castle, projected as competition against her own daughter, who escapes her mother's coldness alone to the mainland, and on the run blindly falls into the arms of the first psychopath who comes along, who pretends to her how beautiful, how warm, how strong, how familiar it is with him, until the mask falls and the bum can't get anything done and even starts a war of roses over ownership of the child. This means a woman who is demanding, out for love, wants to live a wealthy life, doesn't want to work, is dominant, unkind to backtalk, impatient, got pregnant too early, isn't clear about her emotions, has no control over herself, and complains about having had a bad home, which the poor husband and the children have to make up for all their lives.

She sends her whole load of hardship and unresolved childhood onto her husband and child in order to free herself and to pass this negation on to the lives of others. This woman never protects her own children, but only thinks of herself, wants to be celebrated, as the mother animal to be respected forever. The daughter flees, works hard and does not gain any weight. The mother on the island remains, well-fed, a gracious person. A woman who shows psychopathic traits and considers herself irreplaceable.

The do-gooders with the right language
teach elementary school students behavior
swear by non-violent language
meat-free education reverence for the "spice"
facade of politeness, marital sex, Casanova on the side distances
all beautiful animals in the correctness trap !

Tradition displaces religion + language,
culture displaces tradition in my opinion, because some traditions can sometimes be overrated, but culture cannot. I can imagine that celebrities suffer the most, how hard they work to impress the public.

Nobody really knows how to play God
if nobody understands the language of trees
or can interpret the flickering lights behind the lighthouse...!
Obviously I'm an idiot, but maybe there's a chance
that I'm not a huge idiot as I realize
that I learned your language in a real school
and very few people lived my life
are you then a real idiot in my eyes?

My good advice - Be familiar with your own language before attempting to put yourself in the shoes of others! I have suffered so much. Like many people, I am faced with uncertainty before setting off. I have no goal for the future. Bringing out the inner orientation, as well as spelling out facts... is the act of instrumentalizing abuse - says the pedophile in the church!

The language of beating his horse.
Drinking plays on the innermost being.
He always has the last word. The head is buzzing.
The car crashes through the wall. The dog is buried in the lake.
Or suffocated in the trunk.
But the love in their lives never sees the light of day.

You can see that people from Hamburg like to use gutter language, their dialect is unmistakably colored by macho, beer, St. Pauli, I'll just leave it there because it's a party weekend to wind down here, then I have to hurry back, dance with the dolls until I have a heart attack. That's how we know them.

Equality privileges today dull language in the parents' house
no ideas about childhood also uneducated ways of thinking
but everyone is the same again... bullying, everyone calls the same
even primary school playgrounds are called battlefields
and there are deaths too ! The Frisians always buy their playing cards
ready-mixed in the general store. Men usually mix so succinctly.
Women with their finer fingers mix upright.
The Japanese mix with one hand and take photos with the other.
Wizards tend to mix as chubby for the show.
The manual dexterity has always been superfluous, there is the tongue skill.
If in Germany one understands by partnership
something that only sees the dead Prince Charming,
from whose bowels the woman pulls back her damned wedding ring
in detail, but seen as an operation on the man.
Then I save myself the offer of having to marry a German.

No, if someone asks, where my ego is located... I like my belly,
why do I need another one? I don't go crying into the corner
to hide my pussy. It's just a tiny little thing that I put in between
so that I can stay happy inside. Love for yourself is no longer on the
lookout, so people, don't run away because you've missed yourself !

A wimp.... is the one who hopes for the right one,
who will take him out of the parental stable,
who he still beats, cracks, and leaves lying there,
A wimp.... who only comes to her mind again,
when 40 years later she is sleeping almost at the gates of the world in a bed
that is just as soft as him, she dreams having a one-off encounter with man,
A wimp.... who is hit on the left foot by her, rolls away, impregnates another
woman, then hopes for a free kick, the old woman is left sitting alone,
and the wimp goes back to his mother,
A wimp.... who can no longer avoid the laughter,
because he is the laughing stock, and will remain so forever !

I QUICKLY GOT THE PICTURE!
I assume that the extermination of Indians at "Wounded Knee"
was comparatively as cruel as the crimes of the Nazis, and I go on to assume
that each side, whether the American West or our European mainland, has
its medal from the death of Sitting Bull the 1973 massacre, only that I was
not willing to travel through the country with a medal trophy, because I
know the people here, "aunt from America" found out about it from me !

It's true our health most important.
We are responsible for ourselves.
The war we live in, is our own war.
The first step to health is quit the war.
The second step is quit the killing thought.
The third step is hinder the negativity in life.
The fourth step is be patient in suffering.
The fifth step is make yourself strong.
The sixth step is healing over years.
The seventh step is not loose contact.
The eighth step is fight for your right.
The ninth step is keep the balance.
The tenth step is live within the system.
The eleventh step is be aware who you are.

At first, a woman cannot talk about her own rape. She can cry. She has nightmares. She has to regain her body. She has to run away. She must never return. After a long period of trust, she has to gain confidence and start to talk. The whole world has to understand what pain this is for women.
It often starts in the parents' home with every form of violence. That is abuse. Then it will be a nasty classmate from school who will jump on you. Then the family fails and declares the victim taboo. Then the woman will trust a stranger, perhaps an American soldier, and get into his car. Then she will follow some people as a confidant to spend an evening together.

It is a battlefield. Women, don't put up with anything.
The tears are just the beginning !

Flood of the Century ! or Century of Floods ?

It is no longer just... the flood of the century! It is the century of floods!

It is no longer just... the rise of hostile nations.
It is the fomenting of war for WWIII!

It is not just... the use of a weapon of war! It is sheer, embarrassing rape!

It is not just... the avoidance of confrontation with guilt!
It is the stupid rise of schizophrenics!

Was there for a vasectomy, ONCE and NEVER AGAIN!
Vocational school - no longer a learning system, the teacher is at home.
In retrospect, how would I name the vocational school in general?
Place for superfluous provisions for survival with assholes in the:
culture bunker - party bunker - idiot bunker
Protecting the climate or protecting yourself
from it is for those like living a good life,
owning your own home, yacht, bachelor party, accumulating wealth!
Hanging out there and spending your life is better off dying.

Without hope, without sadness. He holds his head down.
Wearily he crouches on the wall. Wearily he sits there and thinks:
Miracles will not happen. Everything stays as it was.
If you don't see anything, you won't be seen.
If you don't see anything, you're invisible.

Steps come, steps go. What kind of people are they?
Why doesn't anyone stop? I am blind and you are blind.
Your heart sends no greetings from the soul to the face.
If I didn't hear your feet, I would think you didn't exist.
Come closer! Sit down, until you sense what blindness is.
Lower your head and lower your eyelids,
until you know what was foreign to you.

And now go! You're in a hurry !
Act as if nothing had happened.
But remember this line:
"If you don't see anything, you won't be seen." - Erich Kästner -

Two days ago before going to bed...
I met this little fellow, the little weasel,
yesterday under the trees in the avenue
a funny little hedgehog ran past me,
and the rainy summer brings two or three snails to my front door every day,
also twice at midnight a big hare ran towards me in the middle of the road,
braked, and ran back the same way it came,
young deer and small roe deer are also hopping around,
they are not afraid of the city, ducks present the crowd of children
in the middle of intersections, I am lying there and the eagle
is waving to the city from the window,
on the roof there a young heron is clattering its beak,
the wild pigeon lets me talk to it, it loves the topic of children very much,
no one is alone!

I am only now learning to understand that after years of friendship, this seemed strange to me. I thought we always exchanged a little or put into words a little. It seems that we both had the same fear!

We both always feared a close, real bond because we know that a relationship can fall apart even after years if just one wrong sentence is said.

All it takes is a misunderstanding and the whole magic is gone. Even after thirty years, there is no guarantee that a spoken word will turn everything upside down. I think we value each other far too much as friends to end it out of the blue in a human way! We are, will be and probably always have been afraid of not hurting the other person ! Life can be strange. But some things just get too close to you throughout your life. It doesn't matter.
Best wishes, your Heike!

Most time Lovers you meet at the corner, would need a better social worker, not to guess, what would be going on when listen honesyt to the inner heart. You have my absolute agreement ! In life, you never give up and hope. Even the really good ones will experience the sun shining for them again ! I also noticed yesterday that when there are a few clouds, all young people, men, wear the same stupid peaked cap. I mean, we all know about the cell phones in front of their noses, even when they are walking, but that they also wear the same thing?

I remember when, 15 years later, I met a brat outside who was talking about her training as a teacher and I told her that I later published a great book myself about social work and education. She said promptly and banally: "Yes, she would already know, because she knows my book too!" I then said in front of her and someone else who was listening: "Oh, you actually read it? "Then tell me if you like it?"

The brat replied: "YEEEEEEESSSSS!"

Uhhhah

Works .... "WAHRE UNSCHULD IN DER LIEBE !"
"TRUE INNOCENCE IN LOVE !" - HEIKE THIEME - YLVA -

Partner coaching... works like this too,
coach and coachee have not had sex for years,
coachee plays with the man, she sends him to a prostitute,
because she thinks that will save her marriage,
the "making love" was thus MOVED to another expensive love island
directly to an outsourced pussy..... quite wonderfully
temporarily well rewarded, no less fun,
in the morning they all get up with her, and in the evening they go again,
they stand with her no less, and then at night he goes back to bed
with the coach at home, and they all go to sleep together.
When people no longer talk to each other.
The feelings of shame outweigh their openness.
"Making love" became embarrassing as they got older.
Then even coach and coachee fall for it,
and the chaos of both idealists begins to falter.

A beauty wilts like a flower, is beauty then power?
Power wilted like a flower. World of vernissages, therapeutic elite,
of spoiled children and grandchildren, grandchildren's grandchildren,
the car keys belong to the daughter,
the power of money thinks everything and everyone is dear,
the born sugar daddy, selfies hang monumentally through the house,
the other people are little caricatures.
Raped women... she can be so badly damaged, abandoned by her family,
and left with nothing, but she can think, but she will flee,
even if she had had a family, and a sister to support her,
and the backing of someone, but then she would start to think,
but then she would flee, her Mega Piggy Family, family would pursue her,
to disempower her, to persecute her, to control her, to denounce her,
but then she would think,
but she would never come back !

You people of today ! Your looks dazzling,
as if you don't take your word for it, want to teach others,
and don't wear your hair down, every city beneath you is drowned,
your faith on toilet paper, no idea what you mean by "up there",
where you can't see anything through the fog,
everything revolves around your navel,
even your greed is immortalized on your face, reveals as a living scar,
and the innocence of youth quickly fades away.
There is nothing, absolutely nothing, that the public is into when it comes
to mother's favorite, as long as the damn time passes.

We see it's a wet summer this year. We had seemingly felt the weather.
Since equally this day, that i gave my lawyer the report with documentation
about just the last four weeks, and my witnessing friend underwrote that,
she immediately called the landlord, and it was how i guessed, they have a
special file for the sick one, with a number to reach any carer for her. She
definitely got told a sharp word, because since tuesday i find peace here
again, and can sleep. That made me relax and fall so deep in calm, that i was
too tired the whole week, like others, too. Two days ago we went finally
swimming again, in that time between wind and rain, and yesterday we
walked outside in that time between wind and rain again. We seem to feel
the bricks between, and nature is awesome happy for the water.

Back to the book, I've wandered between worlds enough to return to the
meaning of diversity and to real life, stop crying and live. For fun... Moving
to beautiful, green Brandenburg is about people getting in touch with each
other and sharing beautiful, colorful customs, coming together across
beautiful, colorful fields, just like connecting the variety of different people
who come from elsewhere in the field. She nourishes unconditionally,
moment to moment. To honor her, to love her, in infinite variety as far as
our temple is concerned, your body is life. You are magic. Don't always
apologize for the fire in you. Experience the stuff of diversity, walk through
it, endure it or maintain style and wait.

Anyone who no longer notices that woman's nature is diversity and that we all complement each other in tolerating this diversity is living without roots! Human diversity refers to the way in which a person learns to learn something from other people on their journey through life! Princesses have to own and condition all the idiots around them as much as they can in order to avoid limitless diversity. If you are jealous of the love of your country and hatred of the other, which you yourself represent, and you forego diversity, you are an idiot. Mental cripples see no diversity, but wish to shine in others, to impress others, in their need to be loved.

Money is a bottleneck, influence has a foreseeable end, power is on the brink, discipline is only for hoarding, pride is thematically derived, removed from change and resources, it hardly means happiness. Our claim is diversity, self-chosen action, a justified view of life !

We met a youngster couple by bike on the long cicle tour back home to France, that i just talked fluid french to them. Then came on the path through the woods a danish gentleman with paraplui very shy, like they are never talk a single word, i told him he should try those american wild berries, they taste delicious. Then some kindful joggers, and at least a whole open minded family with about five fire red hairy children, all so openly, the couple had adopted those many ones from their sister, she was not able to care for her kids. Uhh and again we talked out all things about red hairy kids, the envy of others, intelligence, and envy at school again, and a long tour through life as a teaching how to fight.

They got to know those french guys, too. And one elderly mom with her grandkid they wondered about a huge private place, I told there lives the police chief of town, and that i know them all as very kindful people.

Bye! Be welcome! There is no such thing as bye.
Sentence with nothing. It was probably nothing.
Let it itch. How can your perfect hearing
in its reproduction... empathize with a foreign song?

Saz Evi, I'll build you a roof. Four walls around it. FINE !
And also a room with walls, and a hole in the floor, I'll shit in there.

My father, for his part... a so-called "angry, insulting rapist".
Now it's all clear to me. He wasn't quite right in the head, just because he knew that crimes expire, domestic abuse cannot be proven, the rapes were carried out for him by others, into whose arms he just kept sending me, violence against the child cannot be proven, all close relatives denied the shame for him! HAHAHAHAHA, now it's all clear to me.
That's why, in addition to beatings, he always got this kick in front of the others without being punished. And when I was 14, I exposed him in front of others and laughed at him. That was THE reason to punish me a thousand times over for the insult, so I had been a dirty cunt to my father since I was 14, and even rape was no longer worth mentioning to him. I was not informed of the insulting things that had happened to the monster in his childhood or youth, but I was definitely informed that as a young man he acted out sadistic desires on animals, as my Uncle Ernst can testify, and that he found the burning of Berlin a pleasure while watching it from the roof terrace and smoking a cigar. He's not quite right in the head. My lawyer at the time told me that he was the devil, that I urgently needed to get far away, that he didn't just want to lock me away forever incapacitated, but that he was sending snoopers after me with a file full of information. Hohohoho, all right, then the only thing he could do to me from afar was to denounce me when I was pregnant and steal the child from the confinement bed, and then at 14 to spoil and buy off my son with his lifelong lies about me and lots of money, which was worth 10,000 euros to him at the time. But my son knows that in the future he will no longer need money from bad people in exchange for their control !
Other friends who experienced the exact same familiar fatherly abuse, agree they had it the same. And that coward who is my father is still alive, he is 90 now, and i already have understood the whole thing, about his life long kicks. HAHAHAHAHA you see it is not a whole bunch of family, it is that one single poor old coward. and now I do know, why my laughter was all my life my strongest emotion ever !

Life is a bitch als people would call this, and the German saying is "Who laughs last, laughs the best !" HOHOHO, if i was my own Mom then i would hold my shoulder now. hahahahha hihihihihihi. Wer zuletzt lacht, lacht am besten, i mean a sadist may laugh just good feeling in laughter in his taking pleasure in attacking a defenseless child, but just as long as the truth came out ! then nowadays it is the pleasure on my side ! Once spread, the laughter is contagious.

Life cycle. Water cycle rotates regularly. The lover's worries.
The lover's doubt, Bird collar, Feast of the unknown village name,
The raw emotion of the new poet, The changing pace of civilization,
The growing aggressiveness of the machine. Book a farce of history awoke.
Why do you know the glass of water? How many fantasies floated.
If Americans, with sex and war films in their heads, with eyes as as plates,
stand behind the curtain, from where they see everything behind the veil,
as if everyone were standing on a plate, from the edge the rest of the world
simply falls away steeply, people cannot bear the fact that reality
and having a real choice is out of the question, until someone steals power
with lies, takes away the cherished free world, in earlier times, didn't the
Nazis also rob citizens of all free elections through snake-like speech and
seduction to violence?
People cannot bear the fact that women also marry for money alone,
plan for financial gain, and therefore get divorced,
if someone were to die under their roof, if a love of theirs left the house, if
an accident were to happen to a child, if someone were to take the mold out
of their hand, then one half of the offended people
could either become multiple rapists out of angry hurt,
and the other half could become hermits out of refusal to use violence,
but neither of them ever wanted to win over a new love,
because the picture of the old man would hang on the wall
and be framed there forever, and a large curtain would hang from it,
and not a new village would be founded, might soon bear its new name.
On a single large round plate, there is therefore no room for a new beautiful
village, in which love finds a home !

The fickle person, is he the one you can't count on?
The comfortable person, in keeping with his nature,
doesn't want any deviation. He sees being alone as a cold cave.
He compares being wet with isolation and being let down.
He prevents himself from perceiving wind on cool skin as a clear feeling.
He doesn't even breathe clean air and inhales cigar smoke.
He doesn't hold anyone's hand for fear of being hit.
He doesn't spontaneously meet strangers to give them his best gift.
He doesn't allow his partner to expose themselves in love.
He sees himself growing old and that makes him bitter.
He first judges others because someone stole his childhood.
He settles in places, but to avoid people there.
He doesn't trust the situation of being seen as a person of nature.
He doesn't tolerate a direct word, and simply demands humility from others.
He likes to share his discomfort, like when he talks about the weather. He
feels that the invitation of locals threatens his inner peace.
He gladly accepts any warning from the hater to protect himself.
He lets the people who feel close to his origins stand on the shore.
He goes into nature, but does not recognize himself as nature itself.

What did I always say? I don't want drugs. I don't want a boyfriend.
I don't want tits. I don't want to be a sexologist.
I don't want pubescent brothers. I don't want embarrassing situations.
I don't want to die in the sea of flirting, want no make friends for money.
I don't want a stage name at seventeen. I don't want to be an actress.
I don't want to perform a dance. I don't want a porn in a crochet bra.
I don't want a runway left at the end.
Who says that I need a counterpart to be whole?
Who says that I only want seven children by the time I'm seven?
Who says that I want to have everyone in bed for my career?
Who says that my friendship is a business plan?
Who says that I'll never see the little gray cloud?
Who says that the questions about my ideals are important to me?
Who says that I'm interested in the ideals of others?

Where is the runway? Surely you would know about it?
Would you know about yourself? Who can you stand, yourself?
Who would be able to stand him if not you?
If you look for yourself, you will find it,
it doesn't work the other way round !

You would... get the stars from the sky for me?
without getting me down from the tree? in broad daylight?
hahahaha and not knowing when the torrent would come and where from?
from above or while standing? really all sorts of things,
without your feet in the sand? into the stream, out of the lake
around my tent, away with the fairy?
should stretch my legs, your big fat toes?
and then eat salami on circular plates
with a bulbous glass full of Lambrusco wine?
I SAY NO! I SAY NO! I SAY NO! I SAY NO!

It's not a screw, my love it turns and swirls like water,
you flow here and back again, in circles around it,
like the tides, year in, year out,
you change yourself and the world,
you are patient until spring comes,
and everything starts again anew!
Hold on ! It's not ability in itself.
It's knowing what you can do.
It's said by those who know themselves.
It's believing in what you know.
It's not wasting words on it.
It's applying your ability !

Girls, don't worry, let the boy act as he pleases,
stood like that in front of me, also said, for years she beated him
in the schoolyard, watered him, and sent him to rowing, sauna, music
and self-defense.... "The Biggest Loser are you !"

As I understand it, that school bullies, too, whose pent-up aggression, including that of their mothers, can be directed at everything "else", even at the weird religious teachers, wouldn't bother me at all.
They are also responsible for the desease, the look-away mentality teachers.
Let's see who then "goes off" or becomes terminally ill !
We can celebrate with nature, with friends who are real, and with our artistic skills that we are survivors of this time! Let us be proud that we also know how to heal, especially ourselves. I know the origin of my name, what others lack, as I have seen for a long time! So I'll stop now, make sure that you survive just like everyone else, dear friend.

ALWAYS STAY COOL! Or HOW MUCH DISCRIMINATION
DOES A HUMAN RIGHTS VIOLATION NEED?

Let's start from the beginning! When the bishop says with impunity "Grow and multiply!" in the face of his abused altar boys.
When, in contrast to his chastity, the exact opposite is organized, i.e. a secret swinger club, not with adults, but with children, who are not even asked what they think about it,
the strange question arises, which a mother also asks, whose child was once, quite selflessly and secretly "stolen", "expropriated", in short "borrowed",
who would say like a child used for sex:
"It's nice to do something in a group for sex and to increase faith, but it's no fun always being at the front!"

Shorts are not allowed in church. Weapons are not allowed in church.
But what if the same priests wear hot pants underneath, and the guns are their dicks? But is a woman with mother's breasts, with a calm gait after giving birth, airing the milk bar in public, whose guns ruin everything for a woman?
WHO IS THE REAL PIG HERE?

Question: And what is the name of the one who likes them all? Buddha?
I just mean, from the moment I said the Lord's Prayer, I decided to run away
in a hurry, that was all it achieved. Don't panic. That's a good idea, I also
mean, from the moment I touched myself, I had 1000 moments of
enlightenment. Heaven for cats... oh, it's understandable, VERY
understandable, just imagine if they all thought the same orgasm out of
happiness, just the word, and then it all happened like thunder! Crazy, I can
put myself in a cat's shoes, they're all breathing technique artists.
Well, now I don't feel so alone in the world! Yes, the word is what scares
you. I wish you a good night!

Let me explain you Hamburger Platt ! After talking and say G'bye, guy said
instead of "Mach's gut !" he thought of "Hau rein !" that his Platt worked in
mind and he said "Mau ! Mau !" because we Nordic always say twice "Moin
Moin !" so why not "Mau ! Mau !" it is like "UNO !" and like "Schach
Matt !" this is a good way to say G'bye...! for explaining the wording
"Mau ! Mau !" always said the winner in a children Card game who won.

I'm going to turn myself into a herring, naked, halved, happily gutted,
breaded and fried in the pan, and wait until my tail stands up!
The reading of your friends new book is understandable. It is really a lovely
book, and the story for my senses and thought easy to follow. It is like here
the people who did not grow in the Plattdüttsch would only read and read
the wordings, then understand what is meant. So I have it with skandinavian
languages. Today I was making me sure, how far is my thought to a new
story to write as a story again, and I am content to slowly come to that point,
the basic thought are pretty clear, so I am balanced, and guarantee once this
year it will function. To paint a person just that is my problem, that i am not
aware himself and his face, what ever a laughing face is not easy, but my
theory is the issue of the painting the message and the background must be
funny. When the look on it must make you laugh a bit. It's how you see, you
teach and I will learn the impossible !

My theory you learned from both sides, like i learned too, from that side that i did sport for many years in my life, so today i am totally out of the game meant football, alcohol and aggressivity, too do not want to walk out in the city in nights anymore, because those fools follow their neanderthal willing to find their kicks, this is for a woman, or even anyone who walked in nights outside in the black darkness alone to work or back home, like to see from each place you enter divide those both ways of possibility and better choose the right one, yes, but also see the good in it, that everybody always has the right to choose, you chose to become good at painting and you got it, and writing among other things. I chose to say, that i already know life, the people, the reactions, the dangers, and that long ways to solve problems with such, so keep the distance. Yes it might be the right way to see, friendship for both of us, might be the quiet best way to just keep the individual ideals for each one, and do the best out of it, that this is much worthier for us freaks and better not to try the love card, i would be afraid of it too much, to loose the trust once in just one wrong sentence spoken, and wupps all over, i am much too much overthinking. I am not willing to differ in someones blood, or become one heart for both, then i could not breathe anymore. Yes, for both of us, that is the normal way of living, it is better not to be infected by the normalty as usual, in order to better live in harmony and our own normalty. What is normal ? We are not normed to one. When we both have a normalty and balance found, then we are far better going with this, than behave in what the norm said in reality. What is real ? My life sense is not to belong to someone, like a pet, i may think critical hohoho. Let us stop here, or we find out the theory, why none would love none anymore, or why women would block the men, or no woman would bear any babies anymore. We must learn of each other, but it is not so risky like in a partnership when one single word causes death. Love cuts like a knife, and it kills, uhhhh no in reality most deaths caused by femizides in a relationship, like church said it, "We shall be bonded until death divides us!" I am not willing to marry a sharp knife. Sleep well, and may God bless You ! This is a good distance we use for cooling down and calming our emotions, feelings, and dreaming.

This with you and me is more let the other calm down, more than having to dream always the same about a drowning world, and we do not panic. I know that you see the most films are real, you see the most dreams are reality. This is really good enough to be Good Friends ?!

Traffic light reacts - or traffic light governs?

Accompany an old lady to football with an umbrella?
Or in truth, like Lindner, not even set foot on Sylt anymore,
because of the punks living on the beach?
In 500 days, possibly politics, first the European Championship, 24 days
then 6 weeks of parliamentary summer break, 427 days left
then 3 state elections, results, accusations, 30 days less governing
Election in the USA in November - another 10 day break!
15th Dec - 12th Jan, and standstill in Germany 28 days
359 days left to govern, less 70 Sundays on which nothing happens
plus 10 public holidays, minus 4 bridging days, 275 days left to govern
7 months before an election election campaign, ungoverned,
so minus 214 days, statistical 15 days of illness and absence
minus 35 days of fruitless dispute in the government,
statistical government days 11, minus 1 day DFB final
minus 1 day Germany in the Champions League final
3 days for jet lag from summer time to winter time and back
5 days waiting for a broken government plane
If we are honest, the traffic light coalition
will have 1 DAY to govern until the federal election!
Bad luck if that is February 29th !

THE EARLY BIRD CATCHES THE WORM
Opportunity is the work of one's career. Vanity like a wave of homesickness.
I don't have to say hello. Get rid of bad breath with a joint. Get rid of the
smell of carrion and your nose in the wind. I don't have to fall in love.
Feed the vultures and intimidate. Keeping quiet and lip-reading is isolated
silence. I won't forgive. Describe the one from the front from behind too.

See themselves getting wet from the front. The north as it lives.
I only say "hello" to the one who meets me honestly in the morning.
Why does everyone always want... "the best part of the roast?"
or "the most beautiful thing is far away !" and then
"but you should be happy that the beautiful thing is far away !"
these are all just phrases that are suitable for film titles, but not for real life !

Never search for halluzinations, do not follow the fools,
they invite for a desease lifelong, but leave you stand outside the door,
you find the vision in your heart, not a poison to consume gave that,
what you get is a nightmare,
what left you irritated and addicted,
what brings danger and suffering,
what grows the fear to believe in yourself,
what lets the other talk like brainwash,
what leaves the lonely wolve as abandoned,
what causes more searching, and loosing your way to slow down,
and age coming earlier, and physically get ill, and loose all balance to heal !
The healing of every person,
is to be found exclusively in himself !

If the runaway is the way to survive, so why not ? If the tears of heaven
must be found back, you must find heaven. I know someone who is living
on the road. I have told him - I notice that you're wandering around like a
lone wolf, that can't feel so bad for someone like you! You're not a refugee,
or in a caravan with the whole family. You just have to have fun, nibble, get
drunk. You see them all, the others worry about each other, and you don't
share this with anyone. You can hardly be perceived as someone who just
gets what he wants. For you, there is only the moment. No plan for your
tomorrow. No one waiting for you. No one longing for you. It's a bit strange,
because you still seek closeness to people. It's also a bit believable when
you hear people talk about how a life like this passes and suddenly people
have been homeless for thirty years, as if that were normal. Then carry on
living like that and be happy like a pug in oat straw!

When you run into women you know, just in your thoughts, I imagine you see them all dancing in a row, scantily clad, along the forest path, and you sing from the bush behind them "Fox, you stole the goose, go after them!" or something like that... you'll be able to remember someone! Sleep well through the night of the full moon, and don't let yourself be stolen.

Oh, nooooo
to this day I have never imagined a guy like that,
as if his cock were hopping around, held behind a bush,
first the desire fades, then his smelly feet,
the lifelong fart that binds him, the salty sweat of lack of desire,
and only very lastly, the sight of the guy, and no desire at all.

Just imagine a bath that was too hot,
bright red ears in a towel, a stupid grin,
and he would brush his teeth, then introduce himself by name, ...
and show me a piece of nut chocolate that is stuck between his teeth,
because he knows that from his mom,
little boy doesn't go to bed without chocolate!

I walked naked a childhood long. That i won't love to kill.
I took distance to all who stole from me. That i won't drown mourning.
I took myself as value person. That sexually none had possession.
I first know emotion, feels, hate of others.
That made him think of a better solution.
I am from the woods. That i do know about good health.

None other would have taught me anything as long that nature medicine would exist ! You could say the river flows backwards, when the thin flood is pushed back by the bigger, like people used to be locked up whether in the East or the West for their free opinion and intelligence, today there are still no walls, children are locked up within the four walls.

PUMP UP THE JAM ! Supertraining starts in Mom's womb,
baby trains, moves, grows, walks through the cave,
forwards, backwards, turns back again,
not one single state, altime a change
has nothing to do about what romance feels
to later on be born as strong small fellow !

Love is not a show for superficial peacocks.
Love is not food for the bully for the grave of the unloved.
Love is fleeting like a cleaning product for those who cheat.

I learn non-violence. I love standing up alone.
Mother Nature teaches me. I insist on self-protection.
I am in a community. I do not regret being loved.
I have a nice Sunday. I am certainly attractive.
I have no loss in love. I would be equal in emancipation.
I would recover from a distance without fear.
I would leave no doubt. I advise no one.
I do not regret any decision. I protect my freedom.
I sense my ancestors. I work without stopping.
Fuck that cow Else who doubts this!

Today I saw, sitting in the middle of the high meadow
dragonfly, butterfly, deer and later on the path various eagles,
a young one of them white-headed, the meadow hummed
loudly like seven motorcycles.

Which antiheroes, to put it mildly, "don't get your hands dirty?"
those who grow old, and are celebrated as "dignitaries"
in front of their followers, but are reluctant to admit that they have to treat
grown women, even their own daughter, like dirt, and offer them every form
of violence and prevent them from studying, because they don't adore them?

I didn't want to pay attention to the goings-on at the fair,
I didn't want to look like a drone over the weak and focus
my gaze on their fears, I worked for years
to make the old people my friends, everything is fine, just not everyone
who pays attention to others, because they condemn their silence.
I only celebrate with the CHOSEN ONES !

Sneaked away ! The family at the table, the table is long and empty,
the people are getting older, leaving, they are no longer here,
so often they have repelled themselves by me, all these years,
are no longer a strength of community spirit,
because they are all leaving, what they had in me,
was a guitar that was sold out, was a violin that was taken,
was a dandelion that was wilting, and I had cared for them for so long,
but from so far away today, I say, they can all be cared for,
I would even be the heir who sneaked away from the inheritance !

Imagine me so working as surgery, and one patient would die under my
hands, i would hang me up. Life and Death is so close but dramatically. I
love some people here in the close neighborhood, too. The more empathic
that people are, the more gets in vain when they must pass. AH i don't want
to loose anyone, the one lady from a house aside, said, that this appartment i
live in, was the one of her old Aunt once, she worked 30 years long in the
archieve and she loves since beginning speaking with me about the town
from Middle Age until today. Yes, that is connected to my dreams i always
tell her, then she tells me the real historic background to it. I seem to have a
very clear view to past stories that really happened. Some other elderly or
people were born on one of our islands, they are lovely and feel very much
responsible for other people. But it is as people say important to connect the
history, and the dream to the third the real people, too. In my grandparents
house i found shelter, too, so that i was open to my world to better
understand by dreaming.

Strange, but that's how it's written !

It is often life savers who take your life again.
It is seducers who let you down again.
It is admirers who want to fuck you for their devotion.
It is the brothers without talents who are as replaceable as sneakers.
It is the hurt lovers who suffered financial pain when they split up.
It is violent supporters who are prepared to do anything for money.

But who was the murderer in the end?
It is recognizable as a pathologically narcissistic family,
that is where the perpetrator believes himself in most cases.

That's how it goes in families...
the one, with the empathetic something,
with the looks, with the skills, with the intellect,...
is held up at the end, well prepared and served ice cold,
to be served, to be dressed,
to be confirmed as confirmation of what the family
has thought up, so that they were ultimately "right"!

There are holes in the fence knowing I'll never to be the same again though
my garden death becomes me and sadness births lonely days never
permanent to sorrow me, it's only for a while until my sadness transitions
and I dandelion into a smiling face shines again.

That sounds lovely. I think like you do.
When that awareness of the own death, holds maybe for one day,
but you will watch someone's good eyes,
he is await, until you bear out back what is the sunshine from within,
it explodes upwards from heart, it shakes your heart, then sprinkles
the light energy into your tears, then might want your wings spread again,
you shiver of that erruption coming back,
and wanting suddenly laugh out again,
because life is such a paradoxy !

You caress my infinity that lasts beyond the flesh
my souls fire...how do reach through me
without touch...just the look in your eyes
the heat within, down my spine, teeth on edge...released my flow
trickle effect...spiraling, beaded sweat...between the folds...

You have that same nature like me in you ! That sounds so lovely.
Selflove it's what prepares for such a moment not drown.
Regardless of his personal history of illness or past:
A worker's son meets up with his friends every evening
for milk drinks with synthetic drugs.

Driven by boredom, they go out, beat and rape, kick a homeless person,
push cars off the road, fight with gangs, break into luxury villas, assault the
owner's wife in front of his eyes, leaving a trail of devastation, both
physically and morally. When he kills a woman during a break-in one
evening, he is arrested. In prison, a new type of re-education therapy is used
to rehabilitate violent criminals. The treatment consists of showing films
about sex and violence. The sessions become nothing but torture. When he
is released after completing the radical therapy, his personality is broken and
he himself becomes a defenseless, manipulable victim of his environment...
this shows that any consent to violence, as well as violence against oneself,
never leads to a good end.

The way you walk naked, you are wondering about the eyes ?
The place you take a bath, you are guessing they want your hair ?
The distance from where they look, wanting you the hate to present,
it is the cowards bush, but always too late ! In your battle with the rest of the
world I advise you to side the rest of the world.

Going on foot, secretful, directly, connecting Trains .... light , fast, funny.
If you are such a crossing type, the kinda as i am the border type, always
communicating with each one up to the edges, you are the spider and all will
reach out for you in the center asit, like your mom came from the north.

And friends, and that musician from the east and from the south and me, maybe your one Dad from the east, the other one Dad from the west, the only closer type friends you have is two ones from the country side, and your working mates, north east south and west, how can you manage that ? I would take my legs and run, it is not an easy place to be. I could even not say, you might imagine me easier when make me a woman asit at the swedish border, what swedish border ? i mean there is only the Baltic sea ! i could not sit in the ocean to make you seeing me, to be a Swedish guy for it does not make it easier, you always have them all but they are far, i see you have it exactly like me, those i like are thousands of miles away in all four directions. Close yet far away. We are owning these characters of hawks, we are in thought speed at another place, so it is easy to understand the saying "You can blossom everywhere !" some fly more, the other get off speedy and won't come back anymore, the other ones stay in front of your window truly every day and daytime awaiting you. The birds family is HUGE ! but now i go off or i might become old and blind explaining all this !

People used to say: "Your wish is my desire!"
and "If your panty liner fits well, you'll never have to be afraid again!"
and for father's daughter, her wish will come true,...
but today we say, "One wish changes nothing, one decision changes everything!" that could be a signpost for everyone in the future!

No, people, rockers, birds, loners, ... for everyone!
don't fall down, get up, keep going, don't accept going round in the wheel, because it has to be that way, don't assume that you have to
fall down, get up, keep going, because you become a 'hamster wheel' from which you can never escape !
Decide ONCE that the small branch you are clinging to may
have a thicker branch under the surface that you could sit on,
but you have to look underneath first!
The knowledge of what is underneath
will emerge after years of walking upright on its own!

When you consider how often the Russians have attacked countries
in the last ten years, decimating the population, bombing everything,
and absorbing their raw materials,
Moscow is just the place for barbarians, cyborgs and swamps,
for someone like that the simple church tower in the landscape
is simply the tip of a whale's harpoon that will impale him....!

The fine lady of society earns a good living by selling the children she is
looking after to older men. The educator calls it the carrot and stick
principle, for the participation or punishment of children by sadists.

Like fathers whose children they drill in an art of practice, no matter which
one contains the black-pedagogical message, first you need to perform, then
the art brings you pleasure.

And soon little girls are being advertised online, because of their loss of
attention, admiration, affection and the prospect of easy money, even
without school.

Eternal dependence with a broken will to serve until the end is the result of
this. It has to do with shame.

see, hear, smell, taste, touch, think the direct world of experience

mental phenomena - forms, sounds, odours, tastes, touches, thoughts,
perceptions and feelings

beginningless, unimaginably, complex flow of causes and conditions

with mindfulness and clear comprehension the sense of ownership
dissappears

who we are, our identity is not stable or reliable
the remarkable discovery can be both, exhilarating and frightening

Practice, re-examine, re-cognize, with fresh unbiased eyes, we embark upon a quest to transcend all the ways in which we have limited and constricted our awareness. The world is changing at a tremendous speed, all living beings are beginning to feel this, only narrow-minded people or those who deceive themselves and others continue to follow the same path.

You ask me if I remember you at times.
I remember you when I smell roses when i'm galloping horses
I recall your skin as i touch silk & your eyes as i witness magic
Your hair comes into my vision. When I see a waterfall pouring.
It reminds me of your emotions as I see tides of oceans.

When i took off, my horse decided the way, the horse took off in a hurry,
the one joined his fun with me, my little horse gave me free,
freed from the Planks, cell bars, boundary bars, i fled in that vasteness
a horse told me to, so often, so fast, strong, proud, and stay where i am.

Be gentle as the highest credo, perhaps you are kinda too much of it. Better than not, in real life, your are greatful, and right indeed, that gentleness is the motor, that the believe in humanity, that the exchanges of love, and careful get to know, it is. That's the way it is, when i do not care in every single situation to share, then i loose the wonders of life ! It's just my pleasure. Let it be so dear, water flows and finds its way. Take care !
Yes, the cherry blossom, the apple in the tree still grows !

Drittklassisches, dünn verbliebenes...
für "bessere Vorzüge" angewandtes -
Angepasstes Frauen Arbeitsrecht !
Frau in Arbeit - keine deutsche Errungenschaft !

Third-class, thin remaining...
applied for "better benefits" -
Adapted women's labor law !
Women at work - not a German achievement!

Love is not a show for superficial peacocks.

Love is not food for the bully for the grave of the unloved.

Love is fleeting like cleaning products for those who cheat.

For the lifesaver, love is the fact that he takes your life again.

For the seducer, love is the same as being let down by him again.

Love is for the admirer, whose hurt over separation, whose devotion is only sexual. But marriage is not a German achievement!

Love is for brothers without talents, who are as replaceable as sneakers.

For perpetrators of violence, love is the guarantee of support and assistance, protection only as long as they have made some kind of profit.

I am a woman who speaks her mind.

I am demanding when it comes to working.

I have a talent, so I was of no use at work.

As if I, as a German citizen who is not proud of it, were described as "disabled" for my advantages. That saves confrontation and salary, I don't write on a machine that still allows Nazi keyboards to be used today, people like me insist on working rights. All I need is a Polish surname, and if I come out as "brain-deprived", then the workers - welfare would definitely have a job for me ! But anyone who comes with a semi-skilled social worker's certificate can always thumb their nose at me, even if they don't have any skills, they can and should live out their inflexibility in an authoritarian way, that's what is intended, anyone who does that has a job for life !

If the old love has long rusted, the women stop coming,
it's like with the Chevy that isn't oiled,
everyone ends up an oldie, but not a goldie,
if he's not a civilian, always on drugs,
and under no circumstances can he just call himself Sammi, who opens the
door and gate for him and then for the others,
the guy doesn't see much and has things to do,
no women jump on the threshold anymore,
not unusual remembering the drugged evenings full of ghosts,
"chaos" until you collapse, get it,
hold on, get away, unfortunate, first quickly over "red",
through the back entrance into the castle, then "party in" together,
no question is accidental, not to tell anyone what got into them....???

The Schleswig Castle Museum is spending at least 100 million in state
money and taxes to finance a megalomaniacally large metal reconstruction
of the parking lot at the back of the museum. You won't be able to stop
laughing at the end ! You see at the backdoor in this museum is a tiny door,
from where those workmates from the museum sneaking in, those old
ladies, with their old size beauty with their hanging titts and grey hair, soon
become those sameway Bog body outfit of the one inside of it.

Symbiosis broken up, child theft, one planet, the other next to it,
is not a wreath around motherly love, which is eaten away by worms,
the child is strong, very strong, as the patriarch wants to be.
Mother and child no longer exist, child gone, a skull on the back,
the creature feels powerful, the vow to harm, mother does everything for her
child, who only has distant tears left, but they can flow very beautifully,
the bleating howl of the sheep. The life of two planets.
The love of two estranged people. Mother should feel guilty,
she should drift in the sea as a drowning woman,
alone, like him in the world, of two planets.
Fascists call the child theft A STROKE OF GENIUS !
Let nature be your muse. And not Women be the muse of the Fashist !

My life was not a straight line, was always gentle and smooth,
but help the beast in me, restless by day and by night,
followed the glance of the stars, the beast in me
had to learn to live with pain how to shelter from the rain,
and in the twinkling of the night might have to be restrained,
God help the beast in me, i told them "It was me."
It seems all so close, what they had seen in my cloths,
the small kid in me a teddy bear, that humor was vanished in the air,
of that was i was beware of the beast in me,
hadn't we unclear if it's New York
or New Year !

It doesn't depend on the moon whether we lose weight by shitting !
It's not the soap that dissolves the fat inside us !
A few squats after eating would probably be enough.
It doesn't depend on the neighborly friendship initiation on the look
back over the shoulder that says the other person has known for ten years
that you have been neighbors !

There are no patron saints in the church... for midwives,
who are hardly worth protecting for Catholics, business in their houses are
more likely to be caesarean sections performed in the district office,
none for plants and herbs, none for magicians, juggling chefs,
because the art is described as a lie, and none for ordinary cleaning staff,
not even those who clean naked, none for miracle pills
for hyperactive people because Saint "Rita" hardly helps with ADHD,
none for that very special sausage !

It happens very rarely the fear is unfounded, being afraid of the smell of a
phantom's feet, walking outside, socially phobic, but do feet smell?
I could even have stood barefoot on the coast of Genoa at the age of
seventeen, homeless, but the sisters and brothers of the family, who were
planning their luxury holiday by ferry to Corsica, relieved when they finally
left the sight of me of poverty in Genoa behind them !

I mean, karaoke singing doesn't hold the record for continuous singing,
because glass noodles cooked far more widely,
Asians prefer the spiciness of soup,
failing to pass the driving test is not an issue,
not everyone drives a car anymore,
there is no need for a record holder for gutting fish,
firstly, there is hardly any season, secondly, weather phenomena,
thirdly, overfishing, fourthly, there is no tourism effect,
but because playing poker in the dark
is also widely frowned upon, this doesn't deserve a trophy !
The person who challenges usually has the choice of weapon,
whether it is a sword, pistol, bow and arrow, or axe.
Firearms are only allowed for a limited time.
It may take a particularly to simply kill an animal in a nation of hunters.
That is why it is a state regulation in Canada.
But did the French still serve live songbirds with food in 1967?

The principle of underpants is understood very quickly,
why cover it up, what is so complex, who still wears them?
The underpants are boring as hell, connected to sourdough,
formulated with a warm heart to be wrong, documented by the artist,
certified as authentic, whoever exhibited this, my veto,
because my pants are not a museum for anyone !

Las Esposas, ... the loud ones ! Eating is at home, the marriage is concluded
in the chest, a person who belongs is someone who is viewed with distance,
cannot be defined at all, kept for worse times,
if the wife is good in the Tupperware chest,
most people are in the chest...lessness, if you like sex in handcuffs,
threaten to get your wife out, I also let my dog run around,
without warning him onomatopoeically that he must walk at heel with me,
the exhibition of the exposing woman,
waiting to see how well she would be appreciated.
THANKS FOR THE SWIMMING LESSONS!

In my opinion...
the competition is part of it, as are swimming lessons for children, because children first have to drink so much chlorinated water, spit it out again, and dive down again and again into the piss-filled pool, so that they never forget for the rest of their lives, because nothing makes you harder than drowning in dirt, what a piss mess it was that they learned to "swim" in !

Noodling is, as I see it, excessive hanging out by the pool,
with long legs, tight panties, slightly puffed-up breasts, all lined up in a row,
for the purpose of showing the flesh to those who want to get married
and who never meet "real" women anywhere else in their lives,
due to time constraints or overwork.
These women are extremely sexually under-challenged,
as one assumes, which is why they like to noodle.
You can practically catch them from the pool with your bare hands,
unless they are thrashing swimming noodles!

We go to the water, reach in once, and catch the eel,
like the noodle of the sea, with our arm in the water,
because it is so easy to catch, the point of the matter,
whether someone goes swimming in the rain, or doesn't, it doesn't matter !

She was taken from her family when she was a toddler and raised to be an unstoppable warrior. But for what purpose ?As Saku grows in power and begins to master the four elements - earth, wind, fire, and water - she'll seek answers to that all-important question. And she will learn that there is something beyond the elements - the Voids. If she can learn to bind the Voids, nothing can stop her.

Traveler on long journeys. Dependent on the outdoors. You are definitely not that. You show us the extraordinary fact that people still provide for themselves. You show how a man can manage on his own. You demonstrate the robust stamina of a trapper. You doubt yourself the least. This reflected in your psyche based on all the experiences and encounters you have had.

Enriched as a treasure trove of sun, wind, earth and smells. You are building up a human account that others dream of in romantic films. You have realized that the sunny side of life is unfortunately far too short and rare in a single human life. I firmly believe that you will not forget how to be among people! Of course you know that when you come back to the north you will always get a delicious meal from me, that is out of the question when you have something to report on everything that has happened in the meantime in the short time you are visiting, and on both sides. You see, I understand that your closeness to nature has become your ideal, and I will do my very best to avoid trying to take away from a friend what he has acquired with strong willpower; that is not done in the best of families!

Fitness for adults, woahahahah, with the fun factor, exercise is usually better, imagine the same as an Instagram social marketing doll in an advertising training outfit, with thick-rimmed black glasses that are supposed to look intelligent, and with a smartphone shining through the fitness club. I think that's pathetic. Sitting on the street with no clothes on, showing her pussy as if she were acting out the situation of underage street children, I can never think of a term for those who always post their entire everyday life on a continuous stream, what are they called again? They may be sick, but they still have a name that they are proud of, how sad. Influencer. Term for those who always post their entire everyday life on a continuous stream.

Wrong Brothers ! Against commerce, only butt-fuckery,
fingers in the bum, Infantino, we shouldn't kill football,
we play naked and stretch ourselves out, whether we're men or women,
we show our balls, don't give a number, every document says that
we didn't stay friends, to those who ask for money for a number,
if a fraudster says to me, I'm going to throw money into our relationship,
then that's not my club, and I say "no", don't go into the forest,
and listen to the screaming of those who just turn the corner,
and want to conquer art for themselves, get my rights for themselves,
cook up false names with the brothers, give women false slips of the tongue.

Enjoy the day! ohhh yesssssssss after a hot, then cold shower, second pot of coffee, and a bowl of pudding in the middle of the day, otherwise Saturday is always a lazy day, my dog always gets annoyed by that because he's bored, but the girl has a smoked pig's ear from the butcher before she goes to bed, we've had really mixed weather this year, unpredictable, a week of continuous rain at temperatures of 12 degrees, and the water for swimming was like that.... then a week of collapsing into a coma in the extreme heat, now it's time for cooling down again and a lot of wind, but we're grateful for that, you can feel sorry for the old people, the constant irritating climate, from autumn cold to Spanish desert sun, then constant rain with depressing grey, and again wind that makes you fly away, hot, cold, hot, cold. I'm young enough to say that it's exactly this irritating weather that makes it so special, you stay young ! That's how it is, the older we get, the less we age.

If I go to a... male doctor ONCE more, dude,
I'll hit Lukas on the doorstep, tell him how rape works,
throw him on his own mat, show him the boner,
sit down in front of him with my legs apart,
say, "I'm not here as a sick person!" I'm just here to "fire up the grill!"
I'm one of those really strong women, whose cerebellum doesn't start
to shrink at the sight of him, and I'd even... "grab his balls!"
can then find a male doctor himself.
Anyone who offers something to their children,
goes their own way, takes responsibility for it,
is of course also involved with heart and soul !

The thing of leaving a woman standing there without a word is like entering a museum, feeling at home, and then leaving the woman there like a dog, feeling free, and wanting to say goodbye, you shake the exhibitor's hand, thank the dog, he's there as a model, the main thing is that he's loyal and an unconditional friend, if you were to see each other again, a handshake, the woman's shell that suits her, her lemon-sour face, smiling in honor of it, and leaving her standing there, because no one could express it better than the wish after twenty years, for a happy, single life !

Simply treat the woman like a dog, smiling collectively,
tying her up to the museum guard with a leash, and leaving her there,
for amusement, that is the Schleswig mentality ! It is abuse.

Children don't look at the cloud
and associate it with the end of the world.
Children experience the sound of the sea
and call it just the sound of the earth.
Children feel good
and don't make plans for tomorrow.
Children experience enlightening moments
and consider this to be normal.
Children have to learn from a distance
and protect their own inner world.
Children don't categorize people
and judge them by age, weight and gender.
Children just want to be children
and don't experience places to make noise.
Children are swallowed by the wave of traffic
and the world worries about the paintwork of the car.
Children see their bare, round toes
and don't plan for a high-heeled pump
and a pointy nose, wrinkled looks,
mischievous glee, daily drinking,
the distinction between good and bad,
following the ideal of an individual,
because thinking and forming one's own concepts
are too exhausting for others.

First portrait book almost abstract expressionism
unique cubist illustrations, provocative art
Anthology One: "For those who value nature!"
plus charcoal drawings and portraits
Anthology Two: "Portraits - Easter 2024" - - HEIKE THIEME - YLVA -

Everything used to be better, do you remember what the sentence tells you,
think of my flute playing, another time I remember her
as a prostitute who didn't die, was burned, and then lay in the grave,
not everything was better then, passing the test meant
not drowning when drowning, the music, the flute playing was lovely,
which the lovely maiden still enjoys today, whether the witch lives,
or whether she falls before everyone else.

Today everything is much better than it was then.
Today's youth are ungrateful. Today, think of a different time,
than "back then after the Cold War"; despite prosperity, work, and the booze
and booze, instead of having to freeze, you only had parents who drove their
children out of the stove in freezing cold, and banished them.
In the past BURNED, today BANNED ! The mix of wodka orange or the
none mixing, friends, is today's like Mixing, ahh Mission Impossible !

Poor little mouse I was, escaped from the circus.
I almost died in the fray, won, and lost. But I always had my BROTHER
with me, who picked me up, who gave me bread, who didn't run away.
He didn't have many words to say, either he laid me flat or his face
disappeared. Because when everyone lied until the rafters bent,
they always came from the same nest. And a poor little lonely abandoned
one like me wasn't offered the cherries from the trees,
only what fell for me in between, right?

Yesterday i met a funny aquaintance, you know this was a bit funny the last
two years. I have usually gotten the reciepe of an enzym for my brain, that
small half pill a day since 27 years the same medicine..., and when my
doctor left to the old hospital i followed her, then the new hospital was
build, then she changed over there, i followed her, then she went to retire,
and in two years over there changed the docs for my reciepe with each time
that i was appearing, i always was kindful and presented each one for a get
to know one of my books, but the next time he or she was left again, then
they offered me at another place in the neurologisc corner.

43

A new young russian doctor, and i went over there. He made his view on my reception and awareness, and in the second meeting for my reciepe we had a colossal muscle fight about my warning to him, that i am not that type patient who lays down for him sothat he might get a jump for fun, and all what is my problem depended on a rape that was 45 years before, how i am aware of my own personality, and confronted my trauma enough of times, and may in future only heal myself, no other who did not come to be healed anyway, and i may dream in platttysk if he did not want to understand, and i dreamed of the kyrillic language in a secretful way, ... then he looked me directly in the eyes, said that he is not the slightest interested in that former doctor who gave me that diagnosis, that he is not take this seriously today anymore, and this fact does only exist for the file. Then we were quit, and he said, that i also may start to learn russian for him. Then i gave him my translation of my Art, philosophy and the reading of March into his language and two of my best books as bye bye presentation, and went to search me a local practice to get again usually my medicine from one single place. Then again yesterday i had spoken to my new practice and a female doctor again, she is loyal, competent, and was a chief doctor from the hospital in Flensburg, now started here. She is overhvelmed of all what i did my whole life on my fight of life, and believed everything, sothat was the best way to get over a trauma, that is slowly passing. And for sure without hesitate i may become her patient and recieve my reciepe in future from her. In this waiting room, it was the same adress like my first doctor 25 years ago, when i sat an waited, had a nice talk to a lady aside me waiting, too. She began pludselig open up totally, and opened me her familiar rapist story, the parental abuse, the Art she does, her physically trauma, the depression, and her woke head. That i spoke with her with a parallel knowledge, my Art i do, my best friend Carrie from Canada also sameway, and wups i took her greatest fear from her. She really believed to be fucked by a socalled diagnosis that her brain was becoming smaller by time. I believe that is not true, it was a trick to calm her down. Now i think within our talk she could slightly arrive behind her own secret of life, and lost the fear to shrink in brain, because now when she sees there are so many fucked women like her, that she and her thought is worth it.

So we see, it is every womans or mans special time in his or her life, when the day has come to live with the truth, but first you must have the strength to open up first, to understand the own life, does not mean another explained it to you. If it would be so easy then all could be read on a file of paper how to be healed and it would work, no there is no believe, that is only a weakness of some who follow their leaders, usually to be seen in puberty, but some won't take any step out of it.

Tell me, if you really thought, that any believe was found on such an illusion to read and heal by this, then why tell me, please if i wrote and wrote in my books on 23.000 times about all, healing, experience, learning, teaching, fantasy, creative painting, illustrating, warning knowlegde all types through all decades.... why would then not all those you call the socalled believers not buy my stoff, to heal with it ?? If people are weak, sick, traumatized, they live in their bubble, and the last they would do is read from a clear thinking mind, they are not ready for the truth and most will never be in this life. The youngsters will survive their crisis of puperty soon, but too those addicted to drugs in that strange time of building a brain, will possibly end in sickness a life long, and those people do miss school, work, success, love, selflove, strenght to stand up and fight. Those won't heal by any bible.
It is reality, i know that's why i give the right book to the right moment to the right person as present, i can't open a book bakery, and present my 116 books like book reciepes, and then they came to eat my words. This is the secret of those who fought in life to find their truth, they will always find their way to their truth, when people fought for it, it is undestroyable. But the way to heal things out belongs to the right nourriture, and the moving the body. I had it like that, and it is a fact some short healing happen in seconds but the real way takes a life long. That is why i said that i may be chosen to heal, but the way that others won't be prepared for all of it, makes this risky to give too much of the power to people who would not be able to stand the whole thing to stand their own powers, that is better so to hold yourself back, the most responsibility a person has, is his own, no it is their ability to listen, the way they reflect brings them the path to understand and find their own best solution.

We are all just small humans, with a lot of knowledge and wisdom since 50.000 years in our past of humanity, but we must look into ourselves to understand that, no body needs a leading, all truth is inside, all answers appear when wanted. The ones who don't listen are often the enemy to you, to others and themselves.

RECORD for the YEAR ! TWO MURDER ATTEMPTS in THREE PRIMARY SCHOOL CLASS ! MY COMMENT: NO COMMENT!

Rejected flirting is like being unable to deal with someone,
maybe it's also due to pushiness, jealousy and ignoring the fact
that Mr. Someone is actually in a relationship.

Hysterical morality and idealization is like turning a blind eye to the cruelty of your own children, and condescending aggression against your partner, who is blamed for everything.

Desperately holding the helm in your hand, is like thinking you're pedagogical, and teaching the whole world a lesson, no matter how brutally you ignore the fact that your marriage is in the shit.

Ambition to create a future for hyperactive children, no matter what it costs, to make others suffer, and to show off, to be treated heartlessly, instead of being celebrated and the talented child not being encouraged.

Stalking after the daughter, and spying on everyone, a snooping
that goes to the ceiling, to get rid of the school problem
and to shed the blame for the constant control of others,
when the child's career is finally secured.

The fear of failure, making something good out of agitation,
doubting the system, blaming the teaching staff, as if they and all their children were not fundamentally loved by the teaching staff, who themselves beat up others, torment them, look for the wrong role models.

There are holes in the fence. She escapes and vanishes.
Yet more borders remain. And not all are porous.

A dream of freefom in her heart. But the walls intervene.
She slips through the cracks. To face challenges unforeseen.

I saw her slip through, I looked at her, who was served on a tray,
sent off for rat poison, who was just declared a bouncy castle,
for a lot of fun calling "hello", who was only ignored
until she was persuaded to go for money.

I am sure that all lefties and conservative social democrates now will have
to join together to be warned of the Nazi time and Holocaust that was. They
want more attention now and will protest the right winged. We have to care
of our neighbors, and greet and not ignore only one of them. These cowards
all awaiting to break through every single brick they find in the walls. They
start with the young the most, in psychiatric hospitals, on lower schools, in
lost and abandoned zones, but truly forcibly in those scenes where people
feel "enlighted" and "elitary" to search for their follower promising the even
bigger enlightment if follow the leaders. If people loose now the contact to
the ground, and hide anxiously not to help people in need, and not give them
the needed solidarity, then i say "Good night". Because cowardly people
attack others unexpectedly, which the normal person does not expect.
Who, after fifty years of abstinence in marriage, no longer even knows what
sex is, and already says it in seven languages, still can't see his asshole, even
after forty years of defending his marriage.

Who, after a brazen approach to the fact of falling seriously in love for good
sex, out of the illusion of finally living, and exchanging nail filing,
nightwear, and separate beds for a piece of ass for the most beautiful asshole
in the world, still has dreams of cheating, and therefore swears on love to
run away. So whoever thinks the most disreputable woman of all time is his
angel and falls for it, that she wouldn't even touch him with pliers, if she
could avoid it, and on the occasion she gets the gift of the year, all of his

wife's stolen jewelry, the firm footing of the most stinkingly angry feet,
learned to pull herself out of the mud, the fiercest cat of lost brothers, she'll
break your neck. Finding back to your own humor, is best medicine.
We did not stand our both feet stabil, in order to forget our own ideals, even
the politic wants to lame the whole Europe and future of all.

Who knew that? That capers were simple tadpoles,
but when they saw soupy eyes, on the surface of a dead sea,
they were no longer comfortable being in the water,
so they got into the sauce on plates and the lunch of ordinary people.

Who knew that? That ferrets used to eat radishes,
until they were just round and fat, that's why they were caught too quickly,
and they no longer fit under cars, under which they walk in cities,
that's why they were left to graze in the fields.
Flying capers and round ferrets are also my favorite food, I catch them when
the moon is full, like today, make a nice béchamel sauce with them, and
make rice and meatballs out of the ferrets, the capers look at me contentedly
from the soup bowl, and then end up in my stomach.

How can you be called... Brigitte Hartmann?
That sounds in the room like the disgusting yuck Brigitte comes in...
she only loves herself, nobody wants to touch the sweaty one,
she is even disgusted with herself, only concern is the childhood tapeworm,
still haunts her today, because at least one guy wanted to get close to her,
but he preferred to leave her out of boredom, she takes a big shit
then she was rid of him again, Hartmann, whoever has ever touched her,
Hartmann can count on five fingers !

See, under every shower another lady wanted,
when imagine the one, the other is hunted,
and the waterfall is always taken by the next,
in fact NOT YOU !

People are afraid of not being able to tell someone that they are afraid. People fear the sky will fall if they don't say hello to someone because they might not like them. People worry about hearing someone say in a tired, deep voice over their morning coffee that the whole yoga thing had once affected them in a more peripheral way. People can't allow themselves to be the one they like and hold close to them. People may doubt that they should leave someone as they are, that everyone has to carry their own burden. People don't like to hear someone tell them about their trauma instead of encouraging them to do just as well as you one day!

My lawyer lady and i phoned again....
and we both closed that case for the moment, because she also said, if that sick one now registrated finally in her head to live as usual people do, we may better not make her paranoid with the lawyers warning by landlord, because that might end the opposite and she could really freak out again, but in a way topped than before, i mean that is right, as i said it is good this moment as it is, and i will call her back, when the torture starts all over again. But that lady is informated, and she is still there, when i call her back.

Yes, my theory was that i catched her in the staircase once she was a real freak that time, and she stood right in front of me with one of her people or carers she had, sothat i said it to both, that her terror of nine years long might have to stop now, or she will hear from me !
Yes, and the other point was, that one guy who really passed bye a few of times, and once slept here as guest, witnessing, that he did sit on my couch that morning with his coffee in his hands, and started with his male deep voice talking suddenly loud enough that early that one from up could notice there is a man in my place ! From that day on she held peace. Was maybe the right trigger for her.
Yes, it is a fact that real sick ones like that chick needed different other triggers, as usual people do, it is not the spoken word she changes behaviour. We humans are connected in another way too, that is the sense or the vibes, or tendency, or tension. Yes, my dog is in me, round me and surely gets nervous when something destroys our both peace.

49

Guys, isn't it good to be a social mature being ?
you know what to do in every situation
you know where to get the help you need
you know who is protecting you
you know to be aware of what are your strenghs
you have the courage, wisdom and strength to strive
no matter what today sends my way !!!
Now i have already stoff on 85 pages, that moment the story is just fun,

Yes, like painting, you first collect thought a while, then soon feel a
connected idea, then looking around and see the real story around you and
compare to build chapters, then collect all those new sizes of people you
learned about, and that all gets enough then the story to connect and tell a
little around those things is just for fun, first you have the work in collecting
weeks before, a real book will never be written without the contact to other
people. It shows directly the neighborhood of mine, the typical people in
germany i met, the passing of the past, my stand up in life, those many
many characters i see through wether woman or man, and shows it from the
real side of character, now it is in the start to try to fold out any story maybe,
but could be a reality view again, or the use of real weirdo characters of
people who build a story.

WINDOW GLASS BUILDING BLOCK
It is something very big,
it eats as much as it can,
it pops into the toilet to flush out what needs to be done,
the stream sheds leaves and makes noise,
the lame snail peeks around the corner,
it sticks out very sluggishly from behind the bush,
it scolds, discriminates, devalues the encounter,
it eats at mother's, it avoids looking behind the window glass,
in this case I would only recommend trying it the old-fashioned way,
and better leaving the thick glasses inside,
because you can't see the neighbors through bulletproof glass!

A dragon who liked to breathe fire, spotted a female dragon
and he fell in love with her. She moved into his dragon's den.
The dragon kissed her passionately, with fire from his lungs,
the dragon lady was sweating and had blisters on her tongue.

- Alfons Pillach -

Until we have made peace with our own
death and accepted it, fears will always determine our lives.

Love is the joy of life that knows no age.
The love of two estranged people.
Mothers should feel guilty, should drown in the sea,
alone in the world, 2 planets, fascists call child abduction a stroke of genius!
Let nature be your muse. I was shocked at how many young women's
children are denounced and stolen at birth !

Spoils of a booming economy,
all the wealth & money never down to the teeming millions
- the toiling minions gravity doesn't hold as fortune trickles upward,
that's how society's structured - an elite scheme, equity is always a dream.

PAIRS DELUSION
MANIAC BORDEDOM
UNHAPPY LOVERS
DISFUNCTIONAL SYSTEM
WEAKNESS IN UNIVERSUM
SHARED LOVE IN TWO
DIVIDED LIVES and HAPPINESS
SLAVES IN AN INTELLECTUALITY
SHUT THE FUCK UP
and DIVORCE !!!!

To the locals, the hardcore softies,
those who sweat blood and water in every encounter,
who sniff and trim themselves,
who can't help but constantly have to watch how...
the secret of the river is revealed,
that it must always flow DOWNHILL! LET IT BE TOLD YOU!

I saw a single walking mother today with her baby in her cart, she seemed to be of an age a little too young to be a mother, so about 18 years old, and she was fat like a hippo, and when I saw her again later, she was walking up the soft path for about 100m, she was almost hanging on the ground and couldn't push her cart, she looked like an old person who couldn't move or breathe anymore. That is sad. This is more the tip from me not searching for yourself, Be yourself !

Can you differenciate between the experience, after have had the dinner ?

Mr. So-and-so, be careful, you can fight me, that is well known,
but I propose a solution, you will not forget it !
There were fathers who used to pay a lot to lock up children so that they would have a serious diagnosis and their private lives would become socially nonexistent. My father was one of them, but in 1982 laws changed,
I just had to escape from him, TO THE ASS OF THE WORLD,
in other words to the north, he no longer had that means, my lawyer told me,
only to never return, what a stupid coincidence !

Thanks for the tip, first you get taught about assault
in the family, and deprivation of liberty, then you run away, have a child,
and the slanderers again classify the child as assault
at the time of birth, and deprivation of liberty,
then see how you are left alone as a deer,
that feels and has to experience being alone with it !
Thanks, now I know, how that feels!

52

Lovely ain't ? Am not lazy while i would stand
under the showering waterfall just awaiting that "Love" to the next,
from the last, to the next one in my chain, even without a word,
i am not myself one of them who stand for an illusion, in no silent willing
to be loved, i am not to be changed like a perl in the chain of all others !
A woman is not the towel from each cheap motel to get, and consumed like
a warm summer rain, fantastic and Big Thanxxx to you, my friend, i know i
am aware of my wording, that from some time to time, those words are
shared, and people missunderstand, this is our fate to get to know the people
even it takes some years, to find the trust in someone ! and for your info the
best and powerful shamans teach me to be bold to write their thought on my
body to protest and be uncomfortable and show my anger every single day !

I know what you mean, that i am sameway angry just about the fact, that
there is fight, i would have broken my own bones, in order to tell them to
stop with it. To try hard to get past the anger part, it's like you say, the same
doing since i am on earth my heart lets me pass over, i know, but the mass of
remember causes it takes years. I know it's no solution, to react powerful in
any cases, not to suicide, and sameway not to become aggressor, it's like you
said it, the best way to find things out, in silence with yourself, and find the
strength to strive. Everyone does that !

A child doesn't fall off a church tower, when it has its first friends,
a child hardly loses its mind, if it tries its first joint,
a child becomes an adult, when it goes on its first half-world tour,
a child blossoms, when it has friends all over the world,
a child doesn't have to take its own life,
if it has been in love a few times, a child is no one's property,
so it chooses its true family !

THE KILLER ARGUMENT ! The whole it's "my child", it's "my home"
only leads helicopter mothers even when they object or distance themselves
to chase "the child" out of the family FOREVER!

First they have their feet at the table, then they have no place there,
they should rather not have to learn anything about the truth
about history, secrets, antics, that the beatings when they resist
only serve the "well-intentioned upbringing",
that the healthy sense of humor
only serves the "supposedly sought-after" spouse,
and the family career that has finally been achieved,
if at all, according to the registry "office"
what else are daughters for?

France is stumbling a little. Corona, right-wing politics
little in the fridge, no medicine for the poor, provision for births in decline
state medicine disastrous, staff shortages, no pay rises
poorly paid doctors are emigrating, protest movements
racism as mainstream, environmental pollution......
If the Social Democrats win on Sunday,
negotiations will begin very quickly, improving situation in the country
otherwise, deterioration is guaranteed !

With the brain damage,
the lack of empathy,
the lack of insight,
the dependence on the ego,
the fear of letting go,
the shame of making mistakes,
the distraction from noise,
the lack of positive thinking,
the withdrawal from people,
the resistance to the world,
the loneliness of living alone,
the accompaniment of all knowledge within me,
I endure patiently, and one moment silence,
which runs over me as pleasantly as my skin,
has been like this for a long time and it doesn't need to be more than that !

What America ?
If the American flag offends people, the Americans should get out of their
countries. Cool said, indeed. And what about searching afterwards for that
One Tree with the Free Wind in the Branch ?? I only speak about the loss of
Elvis Presley, and Marilyn Monroe, in former days, the Hippy Movement
was healthier than the basic medical Treatments in America, and i forgot ....
the existing high standard medicine for specialist still for the upper class
indeed against a few more bucks. It will be a Win and Loose in future, like
some will be forbidden to smoke, but some who are the smokers, will eat
the forbidden looser all food out of the frigde and laugh out. The black and
white fotos show the new comer of America's prohibition seems closer than
they wished ! Know that the dregs of human regression will one day devour
their own kind! Has already begun. Of course the sign to see, in America
was able to recognize altime ten years earlier, and easy to read in all good
books. Within this fact, you will see soon more than 50 million Americans
flee ! Unlikely. Not that many have passports. It is like those german nazi
"Reichsbürgers" they also do not own regular passports, it is a SHIT IN
THE OVEN - as you say !!! The people ask me : Not familiar with that
term. Are there any left? I mean the "Reichbürgers" and the "Kookoo Clan"
are poorly said the degenerated dreamers, who want a better time, but lost
the enlightment to it. I am not assuming that 50 million Americans will all
end up in Germany as refugees, whether they like it or not. Just imagine, we
have already had the pleasure of dealing with their soldiers and rapists,
which is unlikely. Now they want to bring their families with them too?
They don't have a home in Europe anymore.

Man eating. Uhh I love U. Fuck he loves me. You love me ?
Uhh I don't care. Love you fuck. Fuck that one damn loves me.
He loves me ? You love me ? Fuck what's Love ?
Yes, I know, we humans are all ONE FAMILY,
and if someone goes under, they ALL go together! HAHAHAHA

Oh, never mind, it's like eating spaghetti, how the woman offers me
to make millions if I include the crazy wave behind her.

At sea as an investment, first pay in 300,000, then she promises me
to make a guaranteed profit with all my audio books!

Eating spaghetti is like, without any liquor, know that
if you drink 1 liter of my piss, you're guaranteed to get healthy,
costs only 400 euros!

Eating spaghetti is also like, according to a compliment,
I should write well, so I should quickly write 1000 euros,
and I'm guaranteed to get 45 books for it!

Eating spaghetti is also like giving a sugar daddy his newborn orphan and
doing anything for his $20 bill. Eating spaghetti sounds like believing a
false document, let's go on a journey, love, and see how friendship pays off?

Favorite sentence in a joint collection of bankrupt banks
"Are you all crazy?" now the tails have been artfully placed on the roofs
financed from red numbers and you still want to admit, over your caviar
breakfast, that you didn't want all of this?!"

"I think of those, who were all known in Israel in 1982,
while traveling through the country, I ask myself how in times of peace,
since a dictator has been massacring, ostracizing, inciting people
who are a little different for 20 years, and now even wants to exterminate
them, using the term "land grab" to dryly carry out a genocide on a tiny
country bumpkin that had no precedent, I think, how many of my friends
from back then, regardless of their origins or color, could still be alive
today?" What do I get for 5k Euros?
Let me think of it.... 1 k Salt ? I know Salt is not easy to get.

Purchasing power, low wages, little work, despite a shortage of medical
personnel but most of the deficit is with the people themselves, whose
health suffers from malnutrition, which can also be traced back to the lack
of food and products on their shelves!

If you talk to everybody in Great Britain,
you do not walk behind the truth, you do not stay behind the curtain,
you understand their strong willing to live healthier, but can't reach the
products, those who keep health. I know that people confront truth,
and think other places are different, the sell, is a mafia selling the own cheap
products, in order to keep the people filled with sugar and fat,
as expensive as mafia wants, those farmers all go plead with that,
the sick consumers have no choice, the sicker they become, the more they
need it as sugar and fat addicted, and die earlier, because at last the sugar fat
addiction is far worser than the alcohol addiction, sure kills slower but
harder. Ah i see, translation problem, i meant What do I get for 5kg of
euros? Let me think... people talk about nature salt, that product keeping the
health, instead of industrial salt, that is pretty much unhealthy. And the
farmers can't sell their products to fair price, these farmers are going
bankrupt, and have to bow the dictate of the mafia.
My "deflowering" was inspired by the question of whether I and the
amphibian, the sow, whose wife I was probably drinking this drink together
with him, it seemed so blue, he actually drank it, I didn't, so I was the
amphibian who got through, what a pity about the man !

Mojave Desert ! Sonny Barger made them upset,
they had to talk about it, the topic about driving license,
they had to keep the principles of law indeed,
was a faking bad and humorless, better had turned from Angel zu Hell,
not needed the Witnesses for anything,
so no Jehova at all, who lived in a slot
as high as the cloud to wait for Jesus came,
in the Lower East Side both were concurrence,
but at least it was God who Personal use announced,
who kicked them out, needed no Jesus until today,
who ever had the longest way to cruise
but made the fault drive a japanese motorbike
way up the hills, in the Mojave desert ?

Who orders that future married couples first have to complete a six-month probationary period? In the modern 18th century, corporal punishment in marriage was no longer common, even if it was still punishable by death, at least the forced imposition of the woman was still common, and then violence was also used if she was unwilling, the woman's cohabitation was finally compulsory, if she was unwilling the woman could be locked up, and only the wealthy son-in-law was allowed, the divorce was only made easier for courtship, and the virgin tax was a must! All of this seemed good enough for the young people to plan a little more for their future together.

Denmark or the North, yes, sayings wordings, but that familiar neighborhood makes it teach us many things, it is our languages have much common, this is altime the difference of the region where the words spoken, the region always variates the meaning, there might be so many interpretations of meanings like people living in the north. That doesn't sound like similar languages, no this is a nordic way to see life, so the region colors our speech, every little difference in the spoken words, but the same meaning, i explain that different people have different backgrounds to speak the same wording, and the region the weather and seasons change, the age of a person, the life lived, the intellectual ability, the ones who speak lesser or are big tellers. The more tolerant we see the other person speak to us, the more we understand each other, this depends not on how much we speak or how we are dressed, some people are often understood by recieve their smile.

To talk to people like that more, i would love to, but i am not rich enough to go on travel, and i am not able to pay that price to walk and wander around with my backpack and dog, and sleep outside like a viking, because my nature is not strong enough for this, to get to know all the lands and people. yes, we are not on the run, but that is good, those who are travelling pay the price of being more lonely because the have still the hardships to survive and be responsble for it alone.

The English do the same. The North to them is that which lies between London and Scotland. ? yes, isn't it funny ??? this is a cute world sight, a different universe in many others ! They also think Hadrian's Wall is the border. Quite bizarre since the entirety of it lies completely within England. I haven't seen it. But my trip to England stopped right after i landed when at that night the officers did not allow to enter without money or any adress, and i think i had no papers, too. We have such a small viking wall here too, the wall that once defended the viking from all the southern wanderer who came for business. It is called the Dannewerk wall.

So when the vikings travelled around, they always brought a little wall with them to feel safe and think of home. nah, that looks in our landscape more like a dam, you may walk on it a while between small trees, and fields to the left and fields to the right, that wall was more i think a symbol, that dam and the wall was used to stop the traveller waves, i think to make them business here at place. We have stones from the GDR wall ! We better do not discuss how many walls we had to have around us.

Should I publish satirical newspaper articles? Can I walk people's dogs?
Perhaps I could also write eulogies for those affected?
I would also sell apples for all I cared? I also played billiards and cards.
Philosophers and poets like me have the least
opportunity to participate in earning money !

If I still try today to justify myself, not to digress into old bad behavior,
like drinking, traveling, gossiping, I would also have the reprehensibleness
of speaking rudely to an official outside,
even from behind where he is standing, "No!"
I immediately say like a shot, "I wouldn't dream of it, I went to the fire
hydrant before, which was less bothered by me urinating !"

In 700 AD, the Welsh were recognizable as soldiers by the fact
that they had the leek on their clothing,
men without leeks had not dived.

It was the time of leek signals, instead of smoke signals,
there were 200-300 million people at the time,
the Arabs invented soap, by combining oil and lye,
burping was the WhatsApp of antiquity,
imitating animal noises does not fit in the city.

At that time, someone had married
the Berlin Wall in memory of the Berlin Wall,
in order to gain recognition in the village,
any means were acceptable, but then at some point the marriage fell apart !

Dr. Pepper (est. 1885) feeling better cont'd their public
domain quietly beneath Walt Whitman's #vss365, 52:

I bequeath myself to the dirt to grow from the grass I love;
if you want me again look for me under your boot-soles.
I stop somewhere waiting for you.

My first run through this story, was my escape from the family,
I was forced to eat their filth, which I did voluntarily, until the day when
I got up again with my beloved grass, and flew somewhere else,
the flight was strange and long, in fact and very strangely I had landed,
but I arrived in my own life !

EVERYONE'S CONSENT means they take RESPONSIBILITY for it!
EVERY CHILD with a strong will knows that the SEDUCTOR
has been designed to their DETRIMENT! Otherwise, THE INTERNET will
be to EVERYONE'S GREATEST POSSIBLE DETRIMENT!

Yes, I know, we humans are ALL ONE FAMILY, whoever goes under by
submitting to American IT companies, also commits political death by
agreeing to prostitution, he is cheating them ALL together!

Same way, as the woman cleverly offers to make millions, whoever translates the insane wave of the sea as "more" for the sake of greed, and includes it as an investment can only pay in 300,000, then the AI promises to make "0" profit with all audio books guaranteed.

How to eat without liquor, know that if you drink 1 liter of his piss, you promise to live healthily, only costs 400 euros up front, because for the sake of the specialness, everyone claims the right to make candy out of shit! Eating spaghetti is also a way of attributing talent to everyone, but friendship is also supposed to pay off, so according to the compliment you should pay good sums for it, as soon as possible, that is supposed to give you potential! Sugar Daddy is a perverted child molester, he shows his often newborn orphans what they lacked in "love" in life, and uses minors to make up for his crappy private life by doing everything for him for his 20 dollar bill. Eating spaghetti sounds like, believing a false document, let's go on a hike, love... but don't get lost in the forest of admirers, yes-men, recognition, affection, partnership, compliments, solidarity seekers, coaching FOREST, and see how friendship only pays off for absolutely nonexistent people or AI systems?

Have you ever tasted it?
Ohh i find the very good Nothing tastes even better than Shit !
Yes, the Shit to eat, meant also the very same you eat,
a month long from one pott. I know the right one, is quiet the one, who eats from golden spoon, then tells you "hello" by "you don't belong to me !"
then runs out the doors and with blown cheek
he she it spits the child in front on its mouth even with
the "Eis am Stiel !" that costed MUCH SYMPATHY !!!
Not in our coastal waters, rivers and drinking water anyway. I know the small stubby middle class performer is not seen as german monument anymore, ... these times passed. That's a fact. But caused not a momument !

Sometimes I think like this you don't want to offer any service,
the whole hall is full of flatterers, get them drunk, all the hypocrites,
just come because there's something for free,
the hot chick doesn't want to have to get married,
I left the cold plate standing, I punched the bear in the chin,
I left the bedsheet clean, it drives past, the sex limousine,
the high voice of the "Oh, God screamer - goodbye!"
very modest as I see it, the child born from it, no cheese soufflé,
no wholemeal bread for the lunch break,
no command for the handmade little housework,
no tolerance for the small dick, it would seem like a waste of time to me,
no need to marry the one who just swiped.

I no longer heal by laying my hand on someone,
but by giving them a full-on smack in the face !

I no longer regret attacking a horse from behind,
but only doubt that it will kick out the back of my head !

I no longer sing to stand out among the crowd,
but rather just happily walk past them !

I no longer drink to summon the ancient spirits,
but rather to not stop laughing at the spirits of today !

I can no longer bear to remember the effect of this,
through a constellation of parents who managed to not speak a word
to each other their whole lives.

I am afraid that I will no longer be able to claim that I have found
the best conversation partner in every animal I have met !

I only decide who I find to be an asshole as a friend,
and not which assholes would like to know me in the future!

I do not study the people who leave behind a bar feeling
in the family circle that can no longer be distinguished
from smoke, murmuring and quarrelling.

I had one first painting book too, did you get this one too ? Some of those
paintings are in both, the size is a tip smaller, but more paintings, yes, now
this proved us, never stop dreaming, never end in a day when there is no
inspiration, once there will come a day, and someone will be happy about
that ! The first, it was done for a very good friend Kali, he did not talk to me
the whole damn life long, but he spoke on the phone for half a year long
about his damn long life., and who is damn sick physically, when his
partnership was in crisis, we spoke and shared our both Art half a year long
intensively, so this book was dedicated to him, he got it to his 55 th
birthday ! this first edition was a kinda show of my dreams. The second was
kinda try to teach me in portrait coal painting.

England has a good political front to the old right winged Tory, the social
democrates won. Poland did the last time the very same !
Let's see how France will function Sunday, Yes, it will be much interesting !
Indeed i remember the French as very proud on national culture things, the
theater, the tourism in the areas with high cooking tradition, they love their
landscape, but still ignorant what depends on nature protecting, and nuclear
power, and they love to present themselves like higher being to all other
countries, they do not talk with anyone who is not owning their language
skills, sothen they won't feed you. Yes, when they will become nazi, they
will loose the whole rest of reputation as holiday land, and loose their
tourism, too, yesss, then they might loose that famous french title in their
contract of France "Liberté Égalité Fraternité" like "Freiheit, Gleichheit,
Brüderlichkeit" this might end and they might sink into the title "Nazi,
Fiends, Military", the people vote, the people get what they are friend too,
yesss, indccd because the East Nazi Russia and China works steadily to
divide each country before every single election, now imagine it is a fact
that USA stands at the same abyss like France.

63

You see, that the sneaky justice in USA already is build by right winged, who now decided officially that Trump has nothing at all done wrong, he enjoys from now on all what he did was in the frame of political order and he won't end in jail never, he is immune against the law. now these Americans do really really know, if that next vote will end with such a crap, they will all loose what was connected to American way of life, for EVER !

Let's hope for a stroke or a heart attack then ? They ought to learn fast, that word "hope" will disappear from that continent.

You think inglash troglodytes need to be influenced from outwith their border? That needs to be reconsidered. We already have enough of them. Those from the Stone Age who live in caves and hardly ever leave the caves, except perhaps alone with ten children they have conceived. They should think about digging their cave passages further into the mountain so that they never see out of them again!

Too bad the vice president isn't popular: an intelligent, black woman is perhaps what they need in charge, They wouldn't let it happen, indeed, because they all know even that they are all sick minds, that any indigenious woman in power will fight for her environment.

She could never stand up politically against a herd of right wing idiots from the Kookoos clan, I wouldn't ! They have been plotting this for decades, designing the system so that the day will come when financial disaster occurs, populism, the sickness of society, the less and less educated people, the media processing that divides people, the land of the elite, the mass without property, slavery in the workplace, the wars they produce to make money not to prevent any wars, the social media to make other countries bleed with fraud and stealing from people they rigorously cheat, all the evil deeds they have plotted to destroy, nothing but evil does it.

The american lawyers with a real mind call this like the socalled soon coming concertina, accordeon and say from that day on that one is truly laid out before all, and no longer just decided or closed, then it would never again be possible to reverse what American dictatorship means !

I have that those mornings when i had a night with relax, and had made a round about the last time and fell in deepness, then those mornings my body does start a let go parallel and i shit once after another time, you see our body is our best friend, so tight to how we feel, he is like our dog, he reacts on how we think or let go.

Walking the dog. Then on the way back she jumped into the little swamp and had a little bath then she got better and I told some asshole on my way back not to point his long arm up to the sky (like a Nazi) with his child in his arms because it was scary for Mable so he had to stop doing that kind of thing, my dog didn't think it was funny, she didn't want to pass the guy who looked like an elitist eco-shithead, he apologized and let us pass, that was finally something, in fact if that happens to him again I'll just raise my voice a little, whatever, you know I never ignore it, I taught him how to behave, it's the rich who need to be taught how to behave, how weird that sounds, yea, and give them a kick, they can have and own and get what they want as if everything that is grown is their garden of paradise. I always think of the elitist, tall, asshole father with wrinkles and grey hair who gave birth to a son and who, like the typical psychopath, thinks he's so damned the center of the world that he never noticed the womb the boy came out of, as if the boy thought he gave birth to him himself hahahahahaha, the clone gave birth to the clone, then why the mother's womb? This fact is why psychopaths never talk to their wives, they ignore each other. Yes, he thinks to himself, "It must have hurt to give birth... why can't I remember?"
This joke was insightful.

A liar uses strange parenting methods
to show the child how easy it is to lie, while still putting on a neutral face.
A liar puts friendship above correct behavior, will describe the cucumber as
climbing material, which doesn't grow as well as his lies.
A liar sells you a Ferrari, and lets the discount fly across the room,
without you ever wanting to buy it.
A liar confirms when he says no, and uses sex to make amends,
even if he says his own wife is dead.
A liar would never mourn honestly, his emotional structure would collapse,
so he would continue to lie, because everything is fine.
A liar knows that he needs people who, out of gratitude for attention, for his
clever alibi believe him in all situations, even when he lies to them the most.
A liar regards every single person as a leftover good-for-nothing, lacks sense
of reality, so that even the second Jehovah's Witness, run away from him.
A liar doesn't like going to work, he sees all of his colleagues as idiots
bathed in innocence who lack marital sex.
Liars are most likely to look for their alibis in dingy dives, where the blonde
wallflower, the pining single mother, or the excluded colleague,
who he thinks is broken enough to serve as a garbage can,
the liar thinks loyal friendship is something
that only those who take themselves too seriously fall for,
let them talk, he says, and he is prevented from lying.
Liars fall for themselves where they are trusted,
then walk up close to one of them,
you can feel it because the lie becomes infinitely thicker.
Liars do everything they can to appear credible,
that's why they send their signals to other liars, the worse the others,
the better he looks, and where the liar places himself, no grass grows.
Liars often claim to be very normal people, in marriage it was normal to
argue now and then, because someone who is deeply involved in lying
has to appear normal.
Liars appeal to people who believe in the illusion of love,
who believe that happiness must be something you can climb to,
because if you believe deeply you don't ask for the truth.

Why do the best women always believe the lie that
the most important thing among friends
is to say that the right man is only one of those
who told the woman in words that they loved her,
and that is precisely why all women fall for all men !
Instead, women should learn and understand that
it is not a question of being told that you are loved,
but rather of seeing that this does not happen,
it was always those who were responsible for botched love affairs
that said that she simply did not deserve love !

My good advice - never get married!
Never let your husband......out of your sight, or he will have dug a hole,
and left everything behind for a climbing cucumber !

It would have been nice if it had been that way, that about before, that about
the lie, Vauvenargue once said that it was always good to talk about
something again that had already been discussed, so that what someone had
said about you or your mother only applied to a love-hungry, unbeatably
naive, obedient receptionist in the foyer, who was supposed to be saddled
with all the sick and disturbed people.
A friend painted a fairy figure, a mix of Red-haired woman, lizard, dragon
or troll ! I have had a dream again being among thousand americans, that
first time i dreamed that five years ago, thinking being living in a small
wooden hutt in my woods, and then on my birthday travelled 1000 american
young people from the south up to me to my party, now i dreamed being on
a travel between all those places in public where are americans to be found,
like one town after another, and i stayed at hotel rooms, with 1000 of people
around me again, and i was in the move from one to the next place or
universe, was a stressy life, ahhh and you see, that my usual troubles in
living was almost those places where i try to live, and so i dreamed being
first found by 1000 people in the lonely woods, and then of course being
amont the 1000 and on the run from one spot to another, that is my innerst
wish to have in my life and living peace !

People in cities are constantly standing and working as if they were underground, which awakens in them the desire, the constant longing, fantasy and yearning for the sunny part of life outside in nature, and being in nature means that you can endure so much noise and stress every day, but react to it in a very balanced and stable way. I look for nature to maintain inner peace and to feel alive without attacks from sick neighbors, it was inevitable that we both met in a world between the two worlds, from that moment on that you hold a young dog baby on your neck and see it slipping into your blood and veins, you change ! Yes, a dog daily, togetherness means relationship, this has nothing to do with love, this is a steady fact, love just comes and goes... ohhh yesss indeed there are many more than in former times, this is funny to see, when i meet outside sick people who know me for more than 25 years in this town, if they did not have suicided yet and still greet me, they seem to feel always that strong love feeling from far, but i cannot fullfill their wish to be their mom, but if you just would need them for a private act, then this is a hard core work to make them understand that friendship only existed by helping each other, but you will see that they continue hide the real contacts. Because in kinda relationship this is too much for them, every encounter with them scratches hard aside the love experience and that stresses them. Sick people cannot describe what they feel, that makes them afraid, this is their tension, this stops only when they hide in their home place, and shut their doors, and those never let anybody in, inside is a mess. A social worker in the children hospital joked with me, i love to provocate the smokers at the huge ash can when i pass and laugh about them, or remind them of the good good breathe, that last one jokes back, he said "We have to smoke, because that is too much cost, if we stop, then they raise the tax immense and we all would go broke !" so i said "Ahh, then it is much better if you all stay sick !" hahahaha
What woman doesn't love the look on her face when she says: "I can do Kung Fu, I love this sport!" while her husband is already doing something else, just as he is deliberately cheating. Mrs. Lavinia from the Westerwald claims to be the smartest in the Westerwald, which is why she makes a career out of a CV of fraud, and can marry any man she thinks is approachable. Love - a double-edged sword. The Kung Fu thing far-fetched.

I have All in All 63 years successful school and working time to show !

Preschool preparation 1 year, Primary school 4 years
High school 11 years, Physiotherapy 2 years
Nursing assistant 1/2 year, Voluntary work visiting elderly people 1 year
Secretary assistant 1 1/2 years, Working with the disabled 5 years
Writing 20 years, 122 publications to date, Publishing and reading art
Single parent 17 years

In a family that abused me, My family still presents me as an idiot !
I have the right to express my objections !
Teachers don't have an epic. The dried-up old teacher,
rigid structures, so unloved that...nobody satisfies her in private,
who hates men so much, that she calls everyone a wimp,
and sees them as fashionably unsuitable, man in front of her like a so-so,
but in secret she stands there with her arms folded, ready to fight,
believing that one day the chosen one will come, who will take her so hard,
that she will hear the bells ringing !

Official teacher an outsider, a sycophant, actually a pervert,
watched the fist-raising virgin girls on the leisure spot,
in his colorless sandals, just an individualist, one asks,

"What's bothering you ?"
"Do you need a piece of chocolate to relieve your stress ?"
"Don't you want to let off some steam ?"
"We're a closed society !"
"Why don't you have a family ?"
"Do you like being the odd one out, without asserting yourself ?"
"You'd love to be the center of attention !"
"There seems to be no interest in the chemical formula,
which probably embodies your entire passion, doesn't it ?"

The person who officially declares "TEACHER",
who comes to the very last point, so to speak, who wants to lead the way as
a chosen example of the so-called integrity of youth as such,...
my "Dear Mr. Singing Club" who...only differentiates, divides,
subordinates, assesses people in a morally questionable way,
authoritatively excludes, prays, judges, tortures,
praises himself in Latin, builds his rights out of misfortune,
promotes right-wing conservative attitudes, gives his two cents where it is
inappropriate, unfeeling, devalues, incites and agitates,
despite embarrassing sexism towards colleagues,
as a long-forgotten species establishes old customs and order.

It is believed to be the last thing the school thinks about when it comes to
the well-being of its students. TEACHER with their PSYCHO SHIT, real
kind of JUSTICE GAP, where TEACHER sees themselves as important:

A woman becomes a thug, who beats young girls,
because a pretty girl stole the pop star from her in her first love.

An informer becomes a hypocrite, who is after a high position,
because he is made false promises, who ignites a never-ending envy.

A pornographer becomes unsuccessful, who puts science above everything
else, because he never shares chemistry with people,
a suppressed sexism simmers within him.

An adulterer becomes an unfeeling relationship breaker, who enjoys the fact
that people with a bad conscience always go home well during the liaison,
and really make a lot of effort in the affair.

A fraudster becomes the opposite of a role model, who collects money that
is not his due, while blackmailing those who know about it, ruining their
careers if it is revealed, and asking poorer people to pay as a rich bogeyman.

FOR ME THE WORD IS
AN ACTION TO PUT THINGS IN ORDER,
TO AWAKE THE LOVE IN YOU,
NOT TO SEARCH FOR THE MEANING OF LIFE
BUT TO CONSIDER IT POSSIBLE !
- Heike Thieme - YLVA -

That's how it goes in families! Not everyone lets that happen to them!
Leave your worries and pain behind before they reach you.
It is painful to have a permanent smile on your face and you miss it in your
heart. Just respect your heart, it's the only one that thinks you are the best.
If you see them happy with others, don't be fooled because that's how they
were with you when they first met you.

Men are also bullies, against their wives,
because they think they are mermaids, who have no legs,
who cannot move, whose only refuge is their imagination,
so they like to be influencers, and the only lapdog for comfort
is the husband's nicknamed Rottweiler, whose great "empire" in four walls,
and a marriage that does not change, perhaps the dog already wore the chain
that once adorned the wife's neck, perhaps he thought her after the wedding
was dry, frigid, or a ghost, who could stand without perfume,
what other women smell like.

This is a loneliness in the neighborhood unit, woman in the house,
imprisoned, not studied, not emigrated, not lived out, not swept away,
not shared in love, not refined, not put aside and revived,
not taken on the debts, not played "catch the fisherman",
not played the fish in the house,
that was left behind the aquarium without water,
woman also enjoys Hitchcock, the whole neighborhood "just fun",
everything according to the rules,
the woman lived there isolated but inconspicuously.

This is the babble, here a welcome greeting for mothers,
which you shouldn't actually say like that:
People, mothers, women don't fall for it. Whoever steals and sits at the table
the smoked fish, the cat has caught it, the mother has the stolen fish with her
kittens at the table and eats what she caught !

Looking at my example, I am in a completely different position
than the parenting clientele, referred to as "The Group",
because I was always so alone, there was only one person for me,
and he didn't even know about me.

I once went into the light, the sky was blue,
the world so far away, the earth in the forest,
the game so close, the mountain was soon there,
I walked along the rock, with long strides and quickly,
flew into the sun, was gone, the stars turned to night,
the nightingale sounded, soon on my feet in the north,
paying no attention to the city.
It has remained that way to this day !

CAPTIVATED, they are EXCITED!
WHAT HAVE YOU DONE TO PEOPLE AGAIN?

Everyone who has grieved knows that.
There are certainly a hundred examples
of people giving their life for the deceased.
One person will definitely get on the wrong bus.
He will hardly find peace alone in the forest.
He will see the dead person fall at his feet.
He would die for love as a clown.
He would take the side of hookers who mourn him.
He wouldn't know whether they should address him as "Sie" or "Du".
He would find his love where it was destroyed.
He would pretend to the world that his heart was in mourning.

It's just right again. During the first WW they envied the lives of kings, -
During the second WW they stole the butter from education's bread, -
Now during the third WW they envy children's innocence and attack them!
It didn't matter whether they raped young women, as Russians, as American
soldiers, or perhaps as Turks. They put all these women into almost lifelong
mourning. That's how it is. But it didn't help anyone. Not even the voyeurs
of society ! SCARED, they are EXCITED! WHAT HAVE THEY DONE TO
PEOPLE AGAIN? Who would gain by sitting on a child and taking his
breath away, without thinking, that he would act with such cowardice,
NEVER do the same to an adult?

They are only confronted when the signal is given to actually try to escape!
The quiet feeling is there again in the evening that the perfect married life
is not going to happen, and the "butcher" on the other end,
"THE RECENTLY "wanted" person, ZACK, turns off a brain?

The evil look that says, "Watch out, we have to get out of here!"
The stupid thing since time immemorial, it will follow the word,
because the REWARD is on CHILD FUCKERS !!
It's a bit like the female version, that plays the traditional cannibal.
You know the female version?

First one of them sticks out her ass.
Then she keeps a man for herself to have fun with.
First she sacrifices one of the children to the pervert.
Then she offers it up, in a neighborly way no less.
First it's enough for the voyeurs for a while.
Then they want to sacrifice grown women.
First they fight for a career. Then they sense that there won't be one.
First they eat their own grandmother as mincemeat.
Then they nccd to spoil their victim.
First they love to play "the helper" in their own, clumsy way.
Then they can't watch their victims run away for fear of loss.
First they have fun, then it ends bitterly.

73

Then their loss has to manifest itself in a bestial way.

Cannibals..... have a death wish, they swear that one day
they will make the world laugh as bad clowns.
Every child was born with a laugh, but they probably had to grunt so loudly
while laughing during the first act that they must have lost
the joy of first love !

The active... evil seek their consolation in the other person,
full of guilt, and longing, and remorse, and the knowledge of love
and the grief for words not spoken, because they know that they are giving
the last straw the knife into the hand of those who are being hurt, with the
sentence "Just be yourself!" in the false belief that as soon as someone
unloved like that leaves, their evil demon will be defeated !

Being faithful in itself is nonsense. If you are incapable of love,
you demand total loyalty. If you long for closeness so much,
you think that a penis is not for resuscitation, but strange as it sounds,
the thing in the test tube represents "Jesus from Andalusia",
and no improvisation fits. So monogamy is absolute nonsense!

Does the housing association have such a good strategy,
put sick and crazy people in the houses and wait,
with Rolex on their arm and link bracelet, the clock hand on the table,
no computer or email, the little email witch on the shelf with a stick,
the board who knows so they can wait
when the whole new wave of incapacitations starts,
crazy people are causing trouble under every roof,
in their Diakonie apartments, but are allowed to do ANYTHING,
all evidence is dismissed, everything is "a bit too thin" they say,
there was no option either to be evicted again,
a good 9 years, and nobody is giving up! The board is already ashamed,
and still no greetings, as if everyone had a dick on their forehead,

No one, no matter how sick, has laid me low,
that an eviction or incapacitation procedure with the aim of
getting people who speak out openly about it out of the way,
using the means of putting an incited sick person forward
and driving them crazy. BECAUSE BAVARIA WANTS IT THAT WAY,
and they FINALLY want to celebrate in COMMON RETIREMENT
on RÜGEN, to overturn a CITIZEN'S LAW, and to incapacitate people
again at random ! A bit of RUDE-SICKNESS but clever,
an "EXPERIMENT" started about 20 years ago.
The umbrella we use to protect ourselves from the rain in the air is our
parents. If we lose them, rain falls on our heads.
The author says. Ahmim.mourad.

If the umbrella is my parents and my love for them is the sun, then why did
their sun burn me almost as hot as the sun? Why has the rain come out of
my eyes in rivers all my life out of grief? Who never saved me from
anything, but wished me every misfortune and emotionally excluded me
from the age of 3, all together? NEVER ATTACK THE SMALL & WEAK!

Your word in God's ear....! You don't know where the umbrella is and the
umbrella doesn't know you. I'm sorry, but you don't know the truth. Or
maybe I'm hiding the truth from you. Remember these words all your life
You don't know where the umbrella is, and the umbrella doesn't know you.
In times of pain and sorrow, I pondered over every twin case, and watched
every twist in the cold heart of a human being, it is my father who is already
standing there before me, as the twin who strangled his twin, and with his
arms hanging, why should I thank him for this?

If it is not the truth, I am sure of it, an orphan will see his umbrella by
chance... only discover it again in another life! If it is certain that you do not
know where the umbrella is and the umbrella does not know you, then
perhaps the man is also designed to hide the truth from the woman, and to
conceal it from the woman when they meet.

Then I say Solong, and I don't care, they won't make me report this sick girl, not to put myself in danger, and as my good lawyer told me, there would be no other consequences for me, this girl would rise to mainjack, and I would have the total problem, but the housing association may have done nothing about it, nothing more than wait for ME to be the one to leave, as a person who is no longer wanted. The easiest way out for them ... and finally to say "it's summer time!!" the association really knows that I didn't have the slightest chance of legally making the sick person follow the advice of her carers, calm down or leave. This program does the opposite. It silences intelligent and public servant people like me. These landlords play God and are paid by the church. When this sick old chick from above wants to exert power over everyone living below her, she knows she had free reign, so she doesn't have the perception to understand without reason why or how senseless her actions are. She doesn't have reason and doesn't have the basic communication skills to respond to my frequent statements. You know, any harm done to one will not reflect on them since they gave others "everything"...but this sick way, SHE IS JUST AN ABUSE OF THE STATE. She doesn't know how people like her are manipulated by it. So I say solong and don't worry and don't be afraid of what's coming and see her tragic noise as just a normal everyday noise that all people have in a house. And I'm not panicking either because this is going to take a long time and I may continue to blame her for it by making a behavior about it public. And most of all, I'm now celebrating a nice summer with good conversations outside and neighbors who actually like me and Mable, and the sick girl won't be the topic of our conversations. I know the worst way to blame an asshole is always to ignore them.

It's not about denouncing people's marriage with all your might. It's more like two fish walking on two legs! As I said, it's daring for a small child to run up to two children, giving them a malicious look, and the same small child at the same eye level sticks out its tongue with an ice cream stick and a cheeky look back. It's also hard to understand how the ugly thorn hedge is designed to cause serious pain to dogs passing by with the cut thorns on the sidewalks, not expecting that the people around.

It won't notice and will criticize the dog for being unfriendly. How unavoidable it is when an ugly woman comes rushing up from a distance, deliberately giving all passers-by, near and far, an angry look, but no one takes any notice of her because they are all busy with their children, walking aside, passing by on their bikes, smiling and fresh from school as friends, congratulating each other on having made it today, amigos! Even a stubble haircut would be of no use to a bourgeois who walks across the street towards you with the intention of running you over in a bad mood, but no one has taken any notice of him since the end of time. How could it even be possible then if a fascist feminist got off her bike and turned into the road so aggressively that people would have no choice but to take cover from someone like that because it is well known that women like that kick hard from the back. How can you tell that sympathy in this country is only given to those who have deeply honest feelings for children and express this out of gratitude to the child. After all, who wouldn't admit that they'd be better off minding their own business because no one is going to do it for them?

Greetings are also possible from a distance and are a sensitive gesture of letting the other person be who they are, as long as they don't ask you for help ! No, we are not all the same, we are individually who we are, but the mass is different, more livable and easier to manipulate, that's why I avoid sports fans. The goal of this crap is to destroy trust in politics, to wipe out the free press, to divide the freedom of equality before the law, to displace popular sovereignty, to prevent the masses from demonstrating and free, open speech, to turn the judiciary into a party judiciary that helps the right, or at least to destroy the basic law of a democratic system. They cause nonstop stress to keep people away from real politics. When they stop waiting for real facts and good plans for the future, they say, "Solong, what a load of crap, a more honest person can maybe be true after all." They sneak in through the back door without society ever knowing what's going on until it's over. This happens everywhere, including in Sweden, but with the last war this will end because after this no one will come here to rebuild everything, that is, our human chance was the only one to finally become mature beings, or everything will end VERY quickly.

Don't do things by halves, and people who do things by halves may retire, but you will not live as long as those who told you to live in chaos are not the ones who will help you put the place in order. Don't accept that the psychos become authoritarian against you.

This is all like everywhere else these days that societies seem to be very polarized for the coming elections, and the percentage is about half right and half left, so for all European countries it will be our future hard work not to slide into right-wing doctrines. America now wants publicity in this way, to show the rest of the world how the right-wingers have already taken the Power Tower, to show how quickly a chosen pig will rip the pages of law and order and democracy out of the American manifesto. This will take maybe a few months and then the book of democratic laws in the American way that we knew WILL BE GONE will be blown up. HERE in Europe it is different, you saw that Poland has now voted the right-wingers off the table, so in England a big rip-off is being ended. The French know what depends on it, as do we all, and the rest of us do not make fun of the French, because this danger lurks everywhere. I SAY these creeps play their games with all societies. They influence the media and cause panic, put people under stress, shock them, spread fake news, fear of the future, hate speech and all that crap. They know which button to push to play and boom, they get more votes because the stressed people just want their peace back and say "Solong" and vote wrong to stop the pressure. They just need a few people in the judiciary and cheat journalism, the right to free speech, free demonstration and so on. Then they have lured society into totalitarianism faster than any normal society would ever experience. A guy like Johnson blamed the English people and panicked them with so much stress that they voted wrong. All it took was a wrong guy.

Imagine this funny picture, when I was in the meadow today with the old apple trees and cherry trees and bee hotels with tall grass and this damn comfortable little thing to lie on, listening to all the birds for an hour in sunshine, between morning rain and evening rain, then I saw this funny picture... a few ugly women came out of one corner after another and all of them were jogging but were not so attractive, as if jogging would make them prettier, and one was a fat little girl in a pink t-shirt jogging step by step, and the mum following behind like a hawk and jogging all around each other... I found it so funny, the ugly ones everywhere and then the older couples, all the women today wearing such African white hats and with them their ancient husbands who had to listen to them, as if the old men were not already blinded enough by life, but their old wives led them home. Life can be funny too, you just have to leave your home. I could imagine that these ugly old and young girls might also have been the OWL's daughters, and she took care of them all.

Money is printed by banks. Material assets are not invisible.
Institutions are puffed up, debts are their own capital. Debts grow.
Citizens work hard, their money - worn out by small money laundering.
Capital income in a triangle, skimmed three times over.

People who bring their money to the bank have fallen for it,
even politics can be financed, by bluffing and the mountain grows,
just because the institutions are largely becoming too expensive,
that the financial world and politics are heading for an abyss !

Nobody will be able to invest 1 cent as long as seed, pesticide and ancillary costs are rising so much and are subsidized. That is well known.
The farmers must be brought together to form large-scale operations,
which give land to the big companies, there is no other way.
The farmers can only survive if they reach a certain standard,
that is the reality worldwide, and there is also a change in thinking.
If you think big, you sell cheaply, that is the only way to find buyers !

I only decide who I consider an asshole as a friend, and not which assholes would like to know me in the future! Anyone who acts like an asshole is educated or ignored. I taught him how to behave. I know that the worst way to blame an asshole is always to ignore him, do you know how i see the sick madame ?

I see her outside standing now called "Gisela" she is aging, and recieves retirement for nothing, no work but handicapped privilege, eats outside that is cheaper, and still thinking "ohh, i am keeping that age of 29" while once her teetch are lying in her rollator and the titts are hanging above... do you know why then i won't choose her to be my best A-hole friend ? because i don't have to !

The Alpha was assigned to the association of those with learning difficulties, if his home has enough money, at least "money like oil" you eat all the time, then the caterpillar says "it's beautiful", while he was chairman it was certainly said that he had distinguished himself militarily, which was later revealed to be fake, his participation in Vietnam, saving the soldiers, was simply made up, which George W. Bush admitted, but he was president of the show and promoted the local cheerleading club. I assume so !

Is the American Dream perhaps a guy who dreams to be Callboy ?
Is it well known, they have fable for Asian, Vietnamese Women,
where they call them Lovers of US-veteran,
or is it the holy day of the Male Fairy, used to find over as Fairy Princes ?
Is the American a passionate fan of Circus Arena and Roman fighting ?
Is that kinda maybe a friend of the octopodes ?
Is the American style of man to cuddle until the doctor is coming ?

In the same way, the question does not arise as to whether the creature that was found in Scotland was a prehistoric monster. The real monster, if you ask the woman at the gynecologist, is the gynecological chair. The woman concluded that such a chair was found on the shore of the lake and that it was radioactive, because the monster for the hole was therefore named Loch Ness. There are also regions in our country where people are not so interested in letters, which is why there is no need for a post office, or a carrier pigeon, or a delivery person who struggles to move his bike everywhere. They are illiterate people who can communicate quite well without that is, in other words. They make music. The transmission of thoughts is also very special in it, it doesn't cost a penny and it helps.

If you are exposed to humiliation, look for the son of the lion, he is the only one who stands by your side.

I know that son is my son. He is one of those sons of the lion.
He is my only family and protective. He is a womanizer as i know him.

Before today I hadn't thought about what life is like without an address?
Sharing mail at collection points. Nothing more.
It's incredibly peaceful - the thought of being completely
free of bureaucracy and official fuss!

Being watched by birds is not as frightening as feeling
the liberation of being replaced by other people's families...
I don't even fear being in the wet, fragrant grass, being plagued by fat snails,
and not being able to lie there in the winter.

I think she might have a strong loss or reality perception, but enough of it
trying to humiliate me since so long. I think she might have a strong loss or
reality perception, but enough of it trying to humiliate me since so long.
She is depend on so much, like medicine, doctors, therapy and eating
outside, that she might even have a big tick in mind, but that made her
depending on so many, that she meant to give her life stress on my back.
I think her biggest trouble she went through the most was her midlife crisis
phase now, wait i had a thought about that chick today.

"NEVER ATTACK THE SMALL AND WEAK!" Your word in God's ear...!
You do not know where the umbrella is, and the umbrella does not know
you. I am sorry, but you do not know the truth. Or maybe I am hiding the
truth from you. Remember these words all your life. Maybe the man is also
destined to hide the truth from the woman and to conceal it from the woman
when they meet. But as innocently small as she appears in her trousers and
high heels and her boyish cap, she is actually estimated to be about fifty
years old, or is already approaching sixty, so she is definitely not as young
as she thinks.

81

She never says hello, is tense, shies away from the neighborhood. The rural innocence she pretends to be is a ridiculous grimace under pure show.

I only decide who I meet as an asshole as a friend, and not which assholes would like to know me in the future! Who is an asshole plays, is educated or is ignored. I taught him how to behave. I know that the worst way to blame an asshole is always to ignore him, you know how I see the sick madam? I see her standing outside now, her new name is "Gisela", she's getting old, getting a free pension, has no job but a disability allowance, eats outside which is cheaper, and still thinks "ohh, I'm keeping my age of 29" with her teeth in her walker and her tits hanging over it... do you know why I won't choose her as my best asshole friend then? Because I don't have to!

In times of pain and grief, I have thought about every twin case and watched every twist in the cold heart of a person. It is my father who is already standing in front of me, as the twin who strangled his twin, and with his arms dangling. Why should I thank him for this? Two fish would rather walk on two legs! If it is not true, which I am convinced is true, an orphan will see his umbrella in passing... and only rediscover it in another life! Then I say Solong, and I don't care, they will not force me to report this sick girl so I don't put myself in danger, and as my good lawyer told me, there would be no further consequences for me, this girl would push herself to the forefront and I would have the total problem, but the housing association may have done nothing about it, done nothing more than wait for ME to be the one to leave, as a person who is no longer wanted.

Easiest way out for them... and to say "It's summer time!!" Society really knows I didn't have the slightest chance of legally getting the sick woman to follow her caregivers' advice to calm down or leave. This program does the opposite. It silences intelligent and public service people like me. These landlords are playing God and getting paid by the church. When this sick old chick from above wants to exert power over everyone living under her, she knows she had free reign, so she doesn't have the perception to understand without reason why or how senseless her actions are.

She doesn't have reason and doesn't have the basic communication skills to respond to my frequent comments. You know, any harm done to someone will not reflect on them since they gave "everything" to others... but in this sick way, SHE IS SIMPLY AN ABUSE OF THE STATE. She doesn't know how people like her are manipulated by it. So I say keep going and don't worry and don't be afraid of what's coming and consider her tragic noise a perfectly normal everyday noise that all people have in a house. And I don't panic either because this will take a long time and I may continue to blame her for it by making a behavior about it public. Most of all I'm celebrating a nice summer with good conversations outside and neighbors who really like me and Mable and the sick girl will not be the subject of our conversations. I know the worst way to blame an asshole is always to ignore it.

But I understand that you have laughed with me many times and cried alone too. This one woman who lives above me is an aging mentally ill person, no matter what her problem is, I don't care. No one wanted to have to share the neighborhood with someone like that, under any circumstances. What I recognize is that she lives in therapeutic contact with assisted living facilities and eats out, never worked. The facility rented her the apartment so she is untouchable and unassailable and with that knowledge she knows that she was allowed to take her anger out on me almost every day and night for nine years in an uninterrupted and humiliating way without any evidence. There is no getting to her. She dresses like she is twenty-one, carries a backpack like her little school bag, carries bags full of candy, crafts, balloons and gifts from her daycare home and pushes everything home in a rolling suitcase.

You see a woman there on the street, when she stands up straight her face has grown old. She is really holding on to this memory of being very young and age shows the opposite, no I know these people from work and they have no idea what their moods, emotions and changes are, they react from one point to another without any reason. They chose me as a buffer zone so the girl can train her emotional outcast and call that her way of healing. The weird girl belongs in the soup, but her age has made it better.

83

She has to accept that she is no longer a pretty young girl. No, so I say, such an old girl does not belong in my soup. But you only get your feelings back when you are far away.

There was the little ring I found in the sand, the pearls shimmered a little blue. And also again an Yggdrasil ring, for the second time in the same place, these are rings that belong to me if I don't take the ring off once. One of the little wolf rings in the ring once had a sharp point and it hurt when I took it off, and I have another ring in my drawer, only made of silver, and it had my son's date of birth and name on it, a silver ring makes my eyes relax. So people see that this woman is also pretending to have a great golden future in a transmigration of souls when she repeatedly manages to drive the people living below her out of the house, openly pretending to be a psychopath, whether in female or male form, they compulsively act the same. Both are chosen by God, but neither senses that they are going up and back to hell. Real friends are simply too smart to behave like bad people! This is how you can tell them apart from normal people. In my opinion and experience with psychopaths, it is easy to see that in this clientele they are in fact real bunglers. Their big dream was over.

When I openly explained to her one morning in the middle of our hallway in the presence of one of her carers, as a neutral stranger, how this person had been humiliating me and making noise for so many years, making my life difficult, even though I had no option to leave here, and I expressed to her several times that I did not want to do anything to her or harm her, with the announcement of consequences if she wanted to understand this correctly.

This is the danger for all people, whether man or woman, if they come into contact with a shiny, bright and big heart, they are all made fools of. And from today on I will leave her lying in the gutter like a wet rag, everyone can smell from afar where the sheep are going. Predators. She should let them tear her to pieces. I have nothing to do with this person!

It is paradoxical when people know that the privilege of life that was given to them because they were not abused, if they were lucky enough to not be on the same side as the victims. On the other hand, this disabled woman is not in control of her awareness of reality, at least her perception is very different from the normal world.

I know many people who know that they do not know the whole truth about everything and do not want to know it. You see, that is human! But in her case, she is trying to turn the tables, to make my life difficult because she is dependent on care and is probably very unhappy with her life because she is not self-determined.

But I still do not care.

Go to Wallachia. You don't give a damn about the city.
You go over to the Silent Land. Past the king's castle.
You stand on the wall, in your robe.
You wanted to avoid catching what was coming from above.
You waved his flag around your ears. You let one go, he had flown away.
Don't you see the lithe women. They went to pick up dung in just rags.
What a king who wore glasses. And those who wore glasses
were punched in the mouth, they called it "Shut up!" by the mob!

SEX horror, but there are no sources that show
that forced chastity with a pussy belt existed,
the whole thing was almost impossible, but in the opposite sense
it was possible that when the man was absent, the professional dildo offered
the most times they were all alone its services to women !

The most frequently spoken sentence
about the idolized brother,
about the son hated by the mother,
about the writer hated by the sister,
about always being put on a pedestal by the partner,
about the longing for peace and quiet,
about the grief for the deceased son,
about the worry for the parents - such driven, trivial nonsense
leads him over and over again to talk
about how he is the eternally unloved one,
and his sister is broken by it, as idealist, trembling with anger and do-
gooderism, her feelings of guilt drive her to fits of tears,
but finally both take themselves far too seriously,
without taking any notice of the other.

People respect those who have money, but honesty and frankness are
appreciated by only a few, when Sister envies my willing to survive,
she is no better than killing me, when Brother envies my ability to laugh at
men, they were carelessly and grey brothers.

There is a big difference, a very VERY big one, because you have not
experienced everything I have in your entire life. According to my CV, I am
unfortunately not capable of being in a relationship. I am sorry about that,
other people say the same. We are not getting any younger, unfortunately. I
say to talented friends, you have certainly traveled far and wide on your
own, thanks to your sound language skills! What I am saying is that I don't
want to start a relationship with anyone, actually with no one at all, and
certainly not with younger men. I don't have a girlfriend or a close friend
who can always see me sitting alone, but I lived this life to be alone, if only
to survive this family that I had inside me, and that works fine, but not in
terms of lasting closeness to one person. If I had been looking for closeness,
I would have studied at a university; I study everything and the world in my
head. I am one of those street kids too; they don't commit to anything. But it
is good for me because someone can philosophize with me.

What I mean by that is, no, I'm sorry, don't come to me, you have to look for someone else in this country, I can't handle a man in this life. You are a lion, my son is like you, and this acquaintance would burn me like a piece of paper, if you don't accept that, our conversation must end here. My door as a friend is open to you.

You won't believe it, but this place managed to heal me and my dear dog protected me. There is no wrong place in this world, there is only you, who doesn't defend yourself. I didn't get sick there, or sicker, but I became a strong fighter. I have a chameleon-like neighbor. As trivial as it sounds, I mean my apartment neighbor. She has been subtly oppressing me for nine years because she is very ill. You would think it's because she hears me talking to my dog, because I have to laugh out loud, and because I live as a free person. I know how important it is to travel. But I didn't have the money for that. I tried everything to defend myself against this person, but she uses her illness privilege to be untouchable.

The fact that I have said all this very honestly is also an attempt to face the facts, and since I am not a blank slate or a simpleton, a speechless blank slate, and have learned my limits, I now also recognize better where other people's limits are and try not to hurt anyone with the help of my honesty. Being clear and honest is the only thing that helps in life. It is not just a matter of surviving on the whole. It is also the case that I recognize that I am not a hero. I am glad that there are real friends. But as long as we do not merge into one another like two birds of paradise, we cannot beat each other's heads in or end up hating each other.

Russia will collapse if Trump does not gain a majority in America. Yes, let us all hope so! I cannot imagine how a large, democratic country like the USA could sink so low as to put a misogynistic, anti-democratic criminal like him on its golden throne; then their country would sink into chaos. Anyone who lives in Israel is full of fear; oh dear, poor Israel and everything there and around it, all the beautiful places that I visited, are gone.

Even when I was at school, it was more important to me to form my own opinion of history and to definitely travel to Israel at some point and confront it, so I dropped out of school and, whoosh, six months later, I was there too. Dropping out of school was the trigger; I was brutally disowned by my family.

Fighting is nature's invitation, Whoever accepts will make progress.
The world has changed. People are starting to think like machines.
We drink water that tastes bad.

Yes, it was definitely a beautiful country. First I saw the beach. Sometimes you see beautiful flowers growing in a bad place. We ask ourselves how? haha, all I know is that sleeping where rats can survive means never losing your sense of humor again, all I'm saying is that where there is enough water, any flower can make it, and a woman can bloom anywhere! Then I lost myself again, feeling a little alone, and cried somewhere in the shade, then I was comforted and taken home as a guest, from there to a beautiful kibbutz. Flowers grow even in France, where at least 100 nuclear power stations are radiating. There are spiteful people everywhere, oh, I don't know, Africa is more of a country of business. Only in Europe is it so deeply embedded in thinking that they secretly make fun of it and yet still benefit from the cleverness of others.

I think women from everywhere have the resource or substance to make this world a more beautiful place because they think about environmental politics. No, I just believed in how I managed to make an upright person out of my only son all by myself. And I'm not in a church. The day could come one day when there could be more peace, then the different religions would realize that it can only work together. That's what I'm waiting for. For me, cultural sites are interesting buildings. However, I think that for children or people who live out on the street, survival is not dependent on a pretty, well-carved 2000-year-old building, but on learning the BASICS of how best to avoid danger.

I imagine it, like an owl in a dressing gown,
like a sausage in a dressing gown,
like a sausage in a pastry shell, like börek,
like three steps to the left, and three steps to the right,
and getting married, dying, everything starting again from the beginning!

If you call politics today, you think of how radically
right-wing they want to be, like Roman games,
including slapstick theater on stage, open-air concerts and disabled players
who are put on display, there is no need for talent anymore,
because whoever denies the truth, also admits that he can't do anything !

The Middle Ages blamed everything, even the cold winters, on women.
The industrial age ruined everything in terms of illness, pollution,
contamination, even the possible future of one's own children
for profit, including the children.
Instagram left everything, even the ridiculousness of the portrayal,
to the stupidest people to become known. Today's world advocates for the
future, and does greenwashing drives petrol cars,
egoists at top speed on the highway, general political situation,
the epidemics, and the threat of poverty,
there is hardly any time stopping the wars,
to do anything about the climatic situation !

But also a Nostradamus who tells the world all the downfalls our world is
facing! Sorry, but I don't think of you as Mr. Doomsday! That wasn't what I
meant, I hope you can forgive me! Do I want to know what will happen to
you or the flower?

Predictions like that scary to compare myself to the flower, if I had all the
problems of rainy summers, cold winters, years with little growth, years that
bear no fruit, poor nutrition, too much fertilizer, etc. I would rather remain
human, because I don't even need an umbrella, because I love the rainwater
on my skin, I just wish for you, my brother, that you grow well and thrive.

No, I don't believe that either, a flower would be the last of all to die. It is a child of Mother Heaven and Earth, who does not abandon her children.

The flower has never asked when it will open its blossom, it simply knows that it will. The flower does not need fruit to bloom, and it is so cheerful that it is certain that if the year is wet, the sun will shine next year. Yes, if the earth died, we would not live to see it, but before that it can swell up into a ball of fire and leave us in a huge torrent of illuminating fireworks, and only then will there be peace, what kind of insect are people that wants to decide whether the good old earth finds peace or not? A lot of worry these days, but who brings me to a church to worship the poor starving body on the cross as a mere fictional character, so that I can carry all its suffering, like that of all the others, on my shoulders and hopefully enter heaven with grace? If only one walk through the meadow, the swamp or under the trees makes me so happy in just one hour that I can find my way home, relieved of everything? If you have spent just one time as a young girl on an island in absolute peace, I will never forget that absolute moment. At first I was surprised at my family, who always stayed in the house and never understood why I always had to be outside, but then I saw clearly that these people could not even see me as a human being, so in their delusion I had become indifferent to them. Only people who have grown up in the way people once inhabited the earth are knowledgeable, and it is precisely such people who will always be our teachers, because they see everything about us, feel it when we recognize, research, learn, and praise us. They feel happiness as if their hearts were flying away with them along with the ladybird. They experience love with every fibre of their being, spontaneously, intensely and lastingly. I believe the knowledgeable are women. They live in an African cave. They are the council of wise women. They know the secret of flying. If you feel it, you don't have to want it, because one day you too will fly. I even believe that men learned to fly before women. Because women are two-pronged, just as firmly rooted in the earth, and they have to put one and one together first. You can travel without leaving your place, but with your mind, the mind is the saddle in which we humans sit.

A single ride in such a saddle from one end of the long beach to the other and you have been around the whole world, so I take care not to fall in love. I recognize my dream horse, as it eked out its existence behind bars, and wanted to go with me because we had promised each other, but then I sat alone on the distant beach and cried afterwards because I didn't have it as my horse, from then on I dreamed of searching this world for my horse, orange in its coat, thoroughbred in its heart, kindness in its eyes. I can't answer that question for you...who is a real woman and who isn't? When I let all my horses go, I had to start out alone, far away, then write all my novels, only then did all the horses fly over me, into their freedom and I belonged to them, so it was no problem for me to finally learn to fly, and it was a woman again, at night in the middle of the unknown city, who showed me the direction of my path. I was thus a nightingale in the starry sky, flying over cities and escaping. I know that sixty years being alone has told me so much about myself. Good, then I am a butterfly that nests in the garden that the farmer neglected because he is stupid.

That was only one travel to Israel, very spontaneously. I was in Crete in Greece, and those guys i was travelling in their bus with me, they were kinda boring to me, that i decided to continue by boat to Israel in 3 days, just to have been there once in life, like my schoolmate and i once wanted to. You know those guys were witnessing that my family abondoned me, and i had nothing to bite, and no place to hide, but they were students, lazy people, one lived in a valley, and so he let me live in my indian tent on his garden, but he never ever decided together with me how things may become better for me, and i was too proud to beg for his food, so i got used to never eat for weeks long, no problem, then they invited me to go on a holiday trip to Greece, and i went on a student trip with them, but they were boring people never speak, and had enoug money spending good times, i had nothing, sothen i left that bus finally. When being back in my tent in that valley they still kept on being ignorant people, even that first days back in Germany an american Soldier had raped me. Nobody cared. That was the opinion of my lawyer i met once who gave me that sharp wording advice to flee as fast as i can, as far as i get to start my new life anew and did never

91

ever come back to my fathers place, who tried to incapacitate me, just in short words said. Jobs that i learned were physiotherapist, elderly care, work with handicapped and asit in the entrance of a socialworkers office, where to help people with problems to get a work or anything to practice on the market, that was from above church, sothey got to know me as person with knowlegde how to treat handicapped, and i was right away giving many advices, but they never gave me a real working contract even not after six years, sothen they sended me home, so since ten years at last i am unemployed, and live from the state with a kinda half retirement but not so much money. I had to do so many works in life without good payment, so that my retire now is not higher than social money. But finally my father told me to give me a little monthly aside of that. I have never gotten the drivinglicense, and not reached university studies, and my spine causes meanwhile backpain when doing hard works, like in a hotel kitchen i did, and cleaning jobs even the same, my back canno more bear that. I was not keen in my future ? and as well in my home town 45 years ago, i was not only once being raped by men, these were three rapes, none in family who gave me shelter and protection. That is why i am little traumatized, but nowadays am over the past. Not keen on my future, was not easy for me, to bear a hard trauma, to change the towns, to never drive a car, not get good paid jobs, indeed, but then raise one child alone, and you still get no good jobs, because then the offices say what to be allowed or not, and that is working without salary, until the child is grown, or i might have nothing to feed my son. With that family i had, the problems had started. I would not have chosen such a path myself. But father was afraid that i would once start in the own life and tell the people how they mistreated me at home, so he tried to better kill me with denounce and stalk and spy my life as long as he gets me behind bars, where he could see me die with, better than that i told the people what was happening in my life. So really there is no family behind me, never really was, but those last ten years i wrote and published my experience, life ideas, path, learnings by life and painted good Art, that strengthed me back to my whole being, and so it is those old people and family rests now existing who are pretty ashamed, never had trusted in me. Complete with university or studies ? not possible, after a rapist trauma.

You are almost not able to join in school classes, with bully, with elitary idiots, with racist, with a-holes that i tried so often in life, but one single day you decide that is was enough, those people won't hurt me or others anymore, that i may really good concentrate on conversation, and own ideas, but not learn to read and remember the learning stoff in studies easy, it does not work, and i have one funny problem, that i am not able to work in business offices, with numbers and plans, and mathematic logic things, because often my brain blocks when thinking in numbers, the secretary must know how to think perfect in numbers, check it and Bookkeeping is error-free, companies demand it.

And it was like my father shouted at me 45 years ago, that if i told anything about familiar abuse, he destroyed me with all that he can, with his influence, money and willing. So he was just a small locksmith in the military, and his spy was to find out everything i did, he wanted to bring me down make me incapacitated, but my lawyer was good enough telling me the laws have changed, that a family has not those rights easy anymore to lock me up for just send me spies I was gone. But later being pregnant my father again spoke to all institutions, and my child was taken away from birht on, that i fought 1 1/2 years to get my lovely son back ! That was the last brick of devlish deed of my father. My son, now is 27, he said clearly, that he fucks on that money from family, they won't bring us both apart, even they tried, to get control on his life too. He does not want anything have to do with them, that was the long side of the story.

You see, my friend, in all that long story was never the chance to live a usual partnership life with anybody. That is why i love more that imagination of a Good Friend and Bro, good my father did not stick in me, the few greenhorns who did it, never mind, meant okay wait until those nightmares end, then flee, i did. Then those flashbacks reappeared, and i was quit. I see it, all this repeats in every single street, some too young end with drugs, some like me end in loneliness, but if i did study medicine with that father, and ended with the top of a job, he still tortured my mind. Some say to be poor but live true is far healthier.

As much as i wanted my life in peace the more that i fled to relationship, that is soo damn stupid but seems to be a triggering technic of mind, like you said it, the more a woman may imagine to be against all Art, she appears the total acceptance. Is it true, that relationship is just THAT ILLUSION ? as lesser that i experienced my PEACE the lesser people act to be in relation to me, the PEACE ? and wait for nobody to open me like a can beer, ant left me empty anymore ? I am tired, and now or soon go to sleep, when the chameleon will be blessing the house peace.

You see, my friend, in all that long story was never the chance to live a usual partnership life with anybody. That is why i love more that imagination of a Good Friend and Bro, good my father did not stick in me, the few greenhorns who did it, never mind, meant okay wait until those nightmares end, then flee, i did. Then those flashbacks reappeared, and i was quit. I see it, all this repeats in every single street, some too young end with drugs, some like me end in loneliness, but if i did study medicine with that father, and ended with the top of a job, he still tortured my mind. Some say to be poor but live true is far healthier. As much as i wanted my life in peace the more that i fled to relationship, that is soo damn stupid but seems to be a triggering technic of mind, like you said it, the more a woman may imagine to be against all Art, she appears the total acceptance. Is it true, that relationship is just THAT ILLUSION ? as lesser that i experienced my PEACE the lesser people act to be in relation to me, so i don't want the PEACE anymore, and wait for nobody to open me like a can beer, ant left me empty anymore. I am tired, and now or soon go to sleep, when the chameleon will be blessing the house peace. I know, I know the plans of American soldiers who know exactly that they can do whatever they want. Similar to the Russian cyborgs. They are always people who rape any young woman because... that's exactly how I remember it, my father sent them after me, the first one "served" me so diligently that I wanted to vomit because of his ugliness, the second one "horrified" and "shocked" me because he went to school with me, the third one tried to "break" me, to whom I clearly told him that he would rather kill me, but I would not obey him. It was only exactly after I had completed vocational training.

At around 25 that I had the first flashbacks - every night for half a year I had the same nightmare that woke me up, I couldn't breathe and thought I was losing all my teeth, at exactly 3 a.m. It wasn't an illusion, it was a dance with the evil.

I call the evil my father.

It was only when I started writing that the flashbacks came back. Half a year later, I almost lost my balance on the way to the post office with my book manuscript in the northern city because my head was spinning violently, but I stood firm. It finally stopped after the 4th book. It was only after I had published 100 books that the flashbacks came back again. I chatted with the wrong person who sparked a series of nightmares in me, showing me what was behind the whole situation of a young woman being homeless. It was disgusting, but I understood the trigger from then on. It is only today, with 122 books, that I understand that it was good for me not to have studied, not to be a famous celebrity, not to have become rich, not to have moved from hotel to hotel, not to have many friends, and that rapists started in my parents' house and everything that came after that will eventually be "history" for me.

Real women don't care about that.
Everyone knows that guys compliment them,
and if you do that, you're doing yourself good.
Because most women realize as they get older,
"She always thought that men were interested in women's inner qualities, ... but they only pay attention to what they see!"
a valuable sentence, hahaha, "I thought you looked older!"
I wasn't prepared for so much pity, hahaha.

I once had a conversation with a Russian woman, when she was coldly dumped and felt ashamed and laughed at, her humane attitude and her whole natural philosophy of equal people suddenly changed. She cursed all and wished death on her love, just as the serious epidemic broke out at that very time and those many died very quickly. I immediately broke off contact with her, saying that no one had the right to make such statements just because of a broken love, to wish death on an entire country, and she was blocked, when it comes to Russian people, I slowly began to suspect that no one should trust them, as they are currently turning into a different kind of person, more like killing machines, cyborgs. They still allow you to speak to them openly, but now there is a sense of threat in the way you look at them. If you have the opportunity to defeat your enemy, you have no pity for him. All of Russia is for sale. Well, and if you tell someone like that, almost directly, the violence he feels, which makes him great, as an educated son of the elite, that you just don't take the young man and pants-shitter seriously for his fantasies of omnipotence because not everyone will throw themselves on the mat for him, then he finds out WHO he is dealing with and you are fundamentally prepared for this conversation and why, then these elite sons become very small and you can smell the shit in their pants! If someone scares me, they will have to deal with ME too!

People who love money are bad. That's why I haven't seen a male German doctor for twenty years. They lie to everyone. In future I will only call them by their first names anyway. and a sick woman who had been abused at home just explained to me that her doctor had worried her by telling her that her "cerebellum was shrinking", what a disgraceful, incompetent piece of rubbish! I told her that I was not entirely convinced that she had such an "illness".

It is true that cruel people do indeed do very bad things, but everyone does it within the limits of what is possible, because not everything is allowed in order to keep things from getting boring! Find out where the ghost train is going. Wise people who observe it are actually right, it is the poor population of those who are not given medical help but are made to look so ridiculous. The girls today, as their physical development shows, are all sexualized at the age of 10, paraded around in front of the neighbors, seduced together, so to speak, then at 15 they are made drunk in front of the eyes of the world to the spectacle of lightning in the black sky at midnight.

Poor Germany! But they don't notice. I have gone my own way, and that's why I know it.

No, I just expressed it in such a way that I refuse to have to save or heal other people who are in need and in emotional distress. I waited long enough for someone to come along who wanted to be healed by me, but no one came. So I decided that if anyone was going to be helped, it would only be myself. I am not a trained doctor, but I am not a person with a helper complex either. No, and no one in this long life has had power over my decisions! I am not a god, that's right. The most that would happen is that a person would like to get drunk with his own kind, then think he is a god, but wake up as a pig.

We remain a mystery in this life.
We are the ones whose features show nothing but calm.
We are the ones who do not turn to anyone when we feel sad.
We heal ourselves no matter how painful we are.
We are the ones who do not surrender to the bitterness of the days, we accept everything that happens silently, then we continue on our path in peace. And peace for our souls when peace is absent from our lives
 The days were the same, the people were the same, so we no longer cared about who stayed and who left. The faces around us, the relationships, the feelings, even the pains, shocks, and disappointments were similar. They no longer moved inside us, i.e., but we began to expect them at any time and from any person, no matter how high his position in our hearts. Our feelings were similar, so laughter took the place of crying. We began to laugh at the intensity of our misery and cry when joy overtook us, lost in the midst of similarities, we did not recognize all of them, we were not attracted to any of them, nor were we repulsed either. It has obliterated every pleasure, taken away every pleasure, killed every desire, and frustrated every attempt.

How many people we lost in our lives because we were too real, honest in all the things we offered. We lost because we were unable to fake our feelings and beautify the way we dealt with them.

We were unable to be fake and friendly. We were clear and frank. We do not know how to pretend and appear in more than one way. We do not know how to twist and turn or assume a character that contradicts our personality. We do not know hypocrisy, courtesy, and opposition to our convictions and principles. We lost because we did not offer anything except from our depths, because we only care about being ourselves. We lost a lot, but we gained ourselves, and this is the most important gain in our lives.

There is a point that a person reaches. We can call it a point of balance and moderation in feelings. Giving the sacrifice. And looking at life in general. Where things do not affect him as before, perhaps because he finally realizes that neither people nor things are constant. Rather, they change and change with time, and this brings peace and reassurance

Therefore, be selective, as selection is an art, and choose carefully what deserves to be within the framework of your life, and beware of wasting yourself and your time in places, relationships or interests that are not yours, do not resemble you, and do not express you. A morning message to your heart..Be optimistic, you deserve life..

Always believe that something wonderful is about to happen.
If yesterday made you sad, what is the fault of today that makes you sad? Smile, you deserve life. A beautiful day brings new opportunities. Put your worries aside and find a reason to smile. Treat your soul with forgetfulness and fill your heart with love, you deserve to live life and enjoy every moment of it. And in the midst of the pain, smile, let the pain realize that it did nothing significant in your resolve, just water your soul with optimism, and give peace to that beautiful heart that you carry within the sides of your chest. Smile, you deserve the beauty of life. In order to achieve psychological peace, you must do the following:

Trust: Delegate your affairs to the one who holds the keys to the unseen. What God writes for you is good. Optimism: The future is more beautiful, God willing. Submission: God destined and did what He wanted, and the best is what God chose. God will relieve her as if she had never been distressed by us, for our entire life belongs to God. Thanks these wonderful long wordings. Very positive. Not authoritive. Very much spoken by heart.

And say, O distant stranger, how do you know distance when you are in your ruin? Did you not see the morning sun or did the stars and the moon block you from life? Oh, winter is snowing. Are you the one who experiences winter on its streets or do you watch it from the train window?

That is it ! The more you live in your heart, and love. The better is distance to be seen. The only one who knows is the one with his wings.

Taking the time to find answers with real questions,
what's stopping you from doing that? but it's going to rain in two minutes! Wriggling around the fact that people on Earth live longer, what's stopping you from accepting that? Trying to explain the world to children, which also shows that they had known it for a long time? Thanking the one who wears the rose on his lapel, what could be nicer than ignoring that?

We have spoken outside, the two brothers, sons from a single parent father and me and Mable, we just spoke about of our theory what was first, the egg or the chicken, then i told them shortsaid my version, and the both had many things to complain, was funny, at least we closed that all in the world wether they are muslim, christian or viking, nature believers or even living in an african cave, and on island they all do believe in the right way they want to, and all things to believe in a better future for their region they live in, and none is better than another not the region nor the people with their believe, one friend's wonderful saying and wording from the Koran made me happy very much. Those both kids, brothers are the kids of the single parent father. It feels good having that understanding between, not many think it over, so that everyone may speak and talk with everyone.

Yes, but what would someone say who only runs in a hurry and for money alone catches the early day like the worm and then hides his deepest, strangest personal problems and runs from one place in the world to another, did he miss like the sun and the moon what concerned him? Did the stars think of him, and did he ever understand the real distance in reality? I mean, that is simply the ability to love oneself and think from the heart, then the understanding of distance is understood, not the seeker of inner peace who by force constantly seeks and looks in another place and never finds himself. Then you saw how he knew the snowy winter better and could live with it from the street, or did he simply notice, "Oh, it is winter when I look from the inside of a train at the snow from my window frame!"

One day, I was walking on a street, and suddenly a storm and strong winds came, preventing me from walking. I found a tree on the side of my street and sat under it. Then I raised my head to a tree and saw a dove on a tree branch, shivering from the cold, with sad eyes. I said to her: Why are you sad?   She told me that I was flying in the air with my son until a strong wind blew and I was fighting the wind. I did not notice my son until after the storm had calmed down, and I looked to my side and behind me and did not find my son. Maybe the storm caught him. While she was speaking, tears were falling from her eyes. I said to her: His son is smarter than his mother. She said: What are you saying? I told her: They took the path of the storm, and you walked against the storm. He was on the other street, on top of a pink tree with beautiful flowers. If he had followed your path, he would have been destroyed by the storm, because he is small and cannot resist the wind. That's why he chose to walk downwind.

I am not famous, but you said it, to write against a storm meant to walk with him, as you see it's true, the novel must be really a novel, so to reach a publisher who brings books in the stores on land.

I see that your style of writing is strong held to real emmigrant, immigrant and travelling the countries, to show how real life may be, with love, familiar bonds, and future planning.

I do hold my thought connected to deeper issue, the heart and mind thing, and the pains and growths. When you write a novel, you must make the reader swim in it like the sea, and then the waves come to him so that he can enjoy his swimming. At the end of the novel, the sun sets on a beach. Through writing, we can control people's minds and we can change their minds. As for the reality that you and Al-Maanat are talking about. People want something that makes them happy, not miserable, perhaps to open a wound again after it has healed.

But as well as the reality meant sameway to me, those talks in most months of the year are the only ones, too, this is a pretty game of conversations and loneliness, but we live here in a strange place of province and town, here connects germany with the nordic, and the tourism from the south, then sea to the left and sea to the right, just a small place in between, so here spoken about five dialects and languages, and all people from far suddenly feel homy here, with much tradition and associations of elderly and people who love to feast and drink among each other, and make their music, or sing in the club. But i was trying but won't belong to people who have money or feast and can't get used to alcohol. These clubs all have their rules, and the outsider and artist like me, would never belong to, not allowed when not been traditional grown up with them and not being the rich class, with house, car, family and job. They like to play so easy come and go, but it is just facade, i would just live here and tell them that i know that town now for real 35 years, and they said "Ask me again when you are living here 65 years, maybe then .... !" but it is not a big place here, so this is harmless, that i am aware the people that i got to know even 25 years ago and after 25 years seen once again i still know them and know their name. They do the same to me, standing right in front of me, telling me "Haven't i seen you in cinema as visitor once twenty years ago ?"- i tell you .... this is a kinda strange place here !

I had a grandfather who definitely mostly painted all those Vincent Van Goghs in oil. The street he lived in was called "Street of Peace - Friedensstraße" and i was over there at visiting my grandfather and grandmother every week, years long, when i got about twelve then i sat there the evening and just asked that one question : "Grandfather, have you been a Nazi ?" and from that on he never talked to me again, he was icy answering to me : "Yes, i was." That other grandfather was violin teacher in GDR, and his wife was playing piano and loved languages. What can i say, that felt in a family often to be held like a stick of icecream in the frigde, they had not such a huge tolerance and attention to kids, we had to function, and i was most time outside and learned to grow from others.

I am just starting a novel, meanwhile almost two in one time, how ever long that takes, that one idea might be good really ! ... yes, from now on i can't get that picture out of my head, see my jobcenter boss there asit with golden teeth from the earrings that i have to pay, still wait for the payment for a painting 100 € and wait for the publisher payment of the 107 €, had given the jobcenter the earnings then i keep from it 30 €.

Now one other Mister" Iwan Thieme "from Ukraine is comedian tells proudly presents himself as a new german citizan, after 6 years files and files and files. My own uncle from the time of GDR over there was called Iwan Thieme. I have a really widespread name, like sandcorn on the beach.

Like a german woman i made just the experience being a true heart, that never got the chance to a working contract, truth is unwanted, they abuse our womens rights with the socalled training of rhetorical traps manipulation bully and fake tellers, and at the last end if you won't stand the missionation of the A-hole then you stand alone, unemployed, ignored, and you might invite them for your reading and five six people who appear, then blowing up the cheeks when i so won't greet them anymore, because i need none slick over my mouth when not want it by heart. I expect to be invited the future, or the things go wrong in future with us, all that what i know for sure it is not the truth of all people in the world, but if those A-holes alltogether just had the AIM to fight me, with the AIM to win over me, then they won't have a damn to do with me, who may believe in peace.

The stupid in Europe always think the same stupidity, that the white european woman is such a silly chick to make her in marriage pretty fast fat, and laugh about her, who had no professional chance, as if she would fit to that level living in a camping waggon to just wait the whole night long how devil sneaks around until she had to fight with, the times still have not changed for women here, but i am far too old to change backwards in times when i was seventeen to finally bring them the stupid chick, that i never have been. But i will care for your word, that it is worthier to keep my money until things like novels will be written, this might be pretty realistic. I AM NOT THE CHICK THAT BELONGS INTO THE SOUP !

Like i can remember that young comedian with the german passport now, he is called like my old uncle from GDR, too. My own uncle from the time of GDR over there was called Iwan Thieme, he died of cancer, uhh he was a huge cigar smoker all the way through ! His motherly name was Kosack. you know the Kosack usually is one from Kasachstan in fromer times, with their pride on horseback, so we directly visited a farm from family when they directly put me on a horseback to go for a walk, and later on it was my wish to work and help in a horse stable in order to ride horses, and got to know the whole world of horse people in my town widespread, those who were Horse breeder, rider, private owner, hunter, veterinarian, helped out everywhere and was witness to a funeral for one old veterinarian, the person, who was often in our stable in lifetime, his horse was HUGE and had a back and form like a swan very funny, when i sat on this one, felt like a sofa and sink in it very comfortably, and also at a horse-drawn carriage wedding in the city, I was asked to bring the bride her flowers.

What i loved was the smell everywhere even the farrier. As very young child i visited that horse stable a few of times, when there lived a Mascot Goat, he stood always in the way and tried to make me afraid by staring at me, but i was not afraid, i messed with him. You know it was that smell of the veterinarian horse medicine in his tiny cupboard place where i had a look in it, the leather fat the liquor for the horse feet, the camphor essential oil, sothat it was easy to me to fold out the thought later on to become a physiotherapist, in order to be taught in anatomic medicine with my hands and empathy a practical healing with therapy most with water and massage.

There, during my training, I became aware of the miracle of realignment, and one of my training partners became pregnant during the training and I massaged her until the baby came; that was a wonderful experience.

I mean i had more the trouble to flee my father afterwards, and to dive under to escape him, so that profession was fast forgotten. Don't be the keeper of everything There are things to let go of and things to finish. Enjoy the changing conditions because freedom is a feeling.

I talked about our friendship to a single good old friend from the town to the danish border, who came along for coffee and cake. He was almost the adopting father to my alone raised child. He is old now and it is seldom see him, because now he started with a slightly dementia, and still drives his car. So we spoke about our both friendship, You and Me, and what you teach me in human understandig of accepting lonelihood and letting things go, to realize self love and the acceptance of the other, and lovely human thoughts you gave me. His best friends is still his long years family from Tunesia. We are all holding together in all difficult times. It is and was our own reliable friendship of someone here in the north since more than 25 years, and because in younger years as social worker, educating in a youth home for school kids after school, he did lead the one 40 years long, his vacancy travels were often to North Africa, so I wrote him one novel once about an old man, on his travel in North Africa by bycicle and on his way back to turn to a monastery, in talk to a wise nun, and then decided to retire from then. But Arne always was in work to do, around his house and still those kids he cared in the tennisclub, so he never read it. Can't tell where they are coming from, because i did not in real meet his friends who live in his town, but anyway we cared for each other. Norma the family mom gave me spontaneously a few wonderful plates handmade and painted. I too collected such plates before. Now i have some wonderful collection, these are lovely plates, who did not break until today Not our friend is from Tunesia, but his friends that family who immigrated many years ago, if you meant Arne's Tunesian friends, who knows, i don't know, just knowing that his father that german one, was communist in WWII and fought strong against Nazis.

They killed him, sended him at last to join the war as canon food. That i didn't marry until today, it is just because i never had a partner before, yeah i often dreamed of Jews from the Nazi time, see them in gas chambers, see them dead lying around in the street, they are real nightmares, i feel it when these unexcepted folks do what they can to keep together or strive in life, they altime kinda paranoid, so they had to be the best in all they were doing, for me it is quiet better to be not Jewish, i had seen enough in my own life, what ever max nix may everybody become happy. If a friend is a good thinker, i say, you are kinda very tolerant young in heart, brilliant in wording, and like you said it a flying bird, that enjoys the wind, that is kinda pure innocence, that migh be disturbed by me at your side, because i am more experienced and not so innocent, that i am that lady fitting to you, you need an unbroken heart, with warmth and steady good mood, and a longing that brings you up to the moon, you need not to try to soften a bigger sister, i cannot change to innocent. Someone is welcome as friend, yes, as long as you return happy to where you live, and maybe want to come back once again, because you loved it.

Filling out certificates for strangers is out of the question. The last time I tried to ask for something online, I only asked for my ID details and 300 euros for nothing. The pretended friendship was a bluff. It's a shame sometimes, like this year when the famous strawberry June full moon was only hidden behind a long band of clouds. No, it was actually 3000 euros. And then the next person who chatted me up asked for the same amount, a full 3000 euros for nothing. And again, someone wanted to introduce himself as a nice Spaniard, and I noticed that he doesn't speak any Spanish. When I offered him something in Spanish, he immediately blocked me. So this time, no request for 3000 euros, hahahaha, so from now on our acquaintance is based on the payment of a sum on my part? He might say: "The dog said to the wolf: "Who are you?" He said to him: "I am a friend of the lion." I say: "Wolf sat on the floor and was awakened by the light when he realized that the dog was his mother who was asking him for help." Nonsense, I'm not asking for money, I hope you aren't either, I just read a certificate can mean anything.

I'm not a bank; my bank advisor would hang me if I asked him for a loan for something dubious again, but it's good that he knows better and tells me that it's an extremely common scam. "When you sit with the lion and aren't allowed to talk about the mouse." Perhaps I'm being very clear and precise about that, but how else could it work? I haven't done anything wrong in our time together. My only great deed today was to forgive myself and my family, and to have written a pretty well-rounded, beautiful basic idea for the book. Oh well, I'm watching again how easy it is for you guys to make fun of people, ok before someone starts with the usual spiel and leaves me with a really big feeling of guilt, I'm afraid I have to step back for today, "Then your victory in the fight against me was no right to prove that the "nice Europeans" are all basically being fooled, I don't regret anything." But then looking back and seeing me as a sister isn't necessary, don't bother, I can manage on my own, so now it's good, first you shoot me down, then you ask again, there's no need for that, I just see you as far away, and you just took advantage of the situation, as is usual online, to abuse my trust, and by the way there is a saying: "Nice is the little sister of shit!" Are you still "acting like a lion"? I said at the beginning that you are too massive and powerful for me as a whole guy, and I am the only one who decides for myself. It annoys me, so I'm turning this conversation off. You have rules in life, so stick to them. I see that there are no recreational gangsters. The network is beyond measure a haven for liars !
 keine Bitte rum 3000 Euro, hahahaha also geht ab jetzt unsere Bekanntschaft auf die Zahlung einer Summe meinerseits ?

Er sagt vielleicht :"Der Hund sagte zum Wolf: „Wer bist du?" Er sagte zu ihm: „Ich bin ein Freund des Löwen."

Ich sage :"Wolf saß auf dem Fußboden und ging im Licht auf, als er merkte, der Hund seine Mutter war, die ihn um Hilfe bat. eine extrem häufige Masche.

„Wenn man beim Löwen sitzt und nicht über die Maus reden darf."

Wrong Brothers ! Against commerce, only butt-fuckery,
fingers in the bum, Infantino, we shouldn't kill football,
we play naked and stretch ourselves out,
whether we're men or women, we show our balls,
don't give a number, every document says that we didn't stay friends,
to those who ask for money for a number, if a fraudster says to me,
I'm going to throw money into our relationship, then that's not my club,
and I say "no", don't go into the forest,
and listen to the screaming of those who just turn the corner,
and want to conquer art for themselves, get my rights for themselves,
cook up false names with the brothers, give women false slips of the tongue.

We don't care who you are or whose son you are. We respect those who
respect us and the rest doesn't matter. No one owes the other an apology, see
you tomorrow. I just have a very bad idea now how it would be possible for
a woman to share an apartment with a man, first sex, then a committed
relationship, then no more small talk, and the woman is simply used for
housework and definitely sent to the kitchen. That wouldn't be my problem.
I'm not suggesting that other people's relationships don't work, but it is and
will probably not be my problem.

There is no safety and there is no end, the word must be heard
in silence, there must be darkness to see the stars, there must be no end to
fully understand what is forever...there must be darkness to be able to see
who you really are...there must be chaos to fully understand it's
consequences. We remain an enigma in this life We are the ones whose
features show nothing but calmness. We are the ones who turn to no one
when we are sad. We heal ourselves no matter how painful we are. We are
the ones who do not surrender to the bitterness of the days, we accept
everything that happens silently and then go on our way in peace. And peace
to our souls when peace is lacking in our lives. The days were the same, the
people were the same, so we did not care who stayed and who left. The
faces around us, the relationships, the feelings, even the pains, shocks and
disappointments were similar in us, but we began to expect them at all times

and from every person, no matter how high his position in our hearts. Our feelings were similar, so laughter replaced tears, our misery and our lamentations. When joy overcame us, lost amidst similarities, we did not recognize them all, we were not attracted to any of them, nor did we feel repelled. It has erased every pleasure, taken away every pleasure, killed every desire and thwarted every attempt.

Don't try to recalculate yesterday and what you lost in it. Once the leaves fall, they don't come back. But with each new spring, other leaves grow, so look at the leaves that cover the sky. Forget what falls to the ground, it has become a part of it.

Never trust the same person who hurt you again. Nature doesn't change. Life is painful when it shocks you with what you thought was good. Compliment those who come to you in their free time. Appreciate the one who gives you your free time. And hold on to the one who pretends to be you...

Don't trust everything you see, even salt looks like sugar. Be who you are, don't pretend. Whoever wants you will love you as you are, with your flaws. Be yourself, everyone has a story and ending. Don't be too sure of your place in people's hearts. People wake up with different feelings every day... Their attitude is constantly changing and their emotions fluctuate in an instant. They can leave you for the most trivial reason and you may be replaced by others.

People are stages, not houses. One stage may last longer than the other. But in the end, you will return home alone. Don't trust anyone. Even the dust you were created from will bury you one day.

I met you here and, in the humorous situation, you were my first lifesaver! Your way of expressing things finally showed me that a man is also a thinker who can do magic. Your work with or on people, in my example, has reinforced the statement that living alone is possible, if only to understand one's life, which is not possible otherwise.

I finally feel like a normal part of society, without being judged for it because people are, on average, jealous. I would often have broken down out of pride because of my waterfalls of tears and moments of sadness; for me, that lasted for 40 years. And it is exactly as you say, laughter, it actually accompanies you throughout your whole life. It calms you down the more you learn about being human. Since I have known you, when I laugh, I no longer fall into the void in which the people around me are all just one piece of water, blurring together, but I see more than ever that the light shines through between all people. Be aware of what I owe you ! You have not succumbed to the drug of life. I finally know the meaning of flying !

The art of living has a title. Don't save anything for later.
Later the coffee gets cold. Later you lose interest.
Later the day turns into night. Later people grow up.
And later life passes. And then you regret not doing something.
When you get the chance.

Life is a fleeting dance, a delicate balance of moments unfolding before us, never the same again. Regret is a bitter pill to swallow, a burden that weighs on the soul with the weight of missed opportunities and unspoken words. So let's not put anything off for later. Let's seize the moments to come with open hearts and outstretched arms to seize the opportunities that await us. Because in the end, it's not the things we did that we regret, but the things we left undone, the words we didn't say, and the dreams unfulfilled.

Have a wonderful day!

Yes, we see so many opportunities that the animal perceives with such passion. The rabbit always runs towards me on the street at midnight because he loves running along it! The ferret likes to go between the houses in the early evening hours to walk under the cars in parking lots. The deer family always crosses the paths together on the circular path in the same places, and then they almost step on my feet. The stubborn loner roebuck speaks to me loudly and still recognizes me seven years later on his paths.

He always stands almost on the paths where people see him standing quietly and fascinates everyone because he is fearless and complains loudly when necessary. The eagle throws himself headlong into love so exuberantly that you would think he started to go crazy until his recklessness became his undoing and females cried for a year after losing them. If we had never taken the path to nature, where would people belong, in the toilet at the train station? Even the tiny blue kingfisher flies out behind the hills whenever I come, shooting from the tree on the left across the meadow to the pond opposite. The heron in the small forest swamp sits up there, and if you just stand there and wait a few minutes, it can fly over your head. You just walk a little way in the woods and five meters further on there is a real eagle sitting on the ground in front of you. I don't want paths that only go around houses, in a nice round curve, past benches and garbage cans where dogs can't run. There are four directions, all of which lead to a little paradise if you just walk long enough! Have a nice evening at home too !

American everyday life is designed for the winning side, the shadow does not exist for them. You always see Americans turning up in huge numbers, there is always shouting, vying for attention, alcohol and fast food are also given out for free for advertising purposes so that the party gets voted for, everything according to the motto "Everything - Everywhere - and Immediately!" One critical look or well-considered statement and you make an enemy. Have you ever imagined a little boy in a soccer uniform who likes to practice his soccer ball in the middle of the night on the front lawn or a little girl who, regardless of embarrassment, goes for a pee on the lawn in front of the house? That doesn't exist in the USA, it's almost against the law.

The latest Western threat!
The "progress" of the "West" soon a faint memory...!
I remember, when my child was small, I could fill my shopping cart
for 2 weeks' shopping for 50 Deutschmarks.
10 years later the Euro came along, you could get half the goods for 50 €.
20 years later today, for 50 euros you can only get basic bread, sausage, cheese, toilet paper, milk and coffee, vegetables from the market, that's it!

And then America wants to make the brilliant suggestion
that we Europeans would....no longer trade with them,
and that tariffs would prevent any sales!

We could hear the flutter miles away, hundreds of birds flapped their wings
and flew in fascinating formations, when the air was clean and sky pristine
decades ago, now it's only stories and memories
of melodic lines and chorus of birdsong.

That's for your information! Don't make any effort.
As if you were interested in the "niceness" of European women,
whose mothers only cook with water, whose fathers recently washed the
dishes, whose children see no future for their pensions.
German women in % only have 1 child, if at all,
millions of people are leaving the church because of abuse,
politics is not child-friendly, traffic is not pedestrian-friendly,
education is not... adapted to new conditions.
If you had ever shown true commitment to the well-being of our born
children, ... instead of taking after us early on, who knows?

Is there a basic right to clean drinking water?
But in fact 1000 children under 5 die EVERY DAY from unclean water,
in cities with ostentatious construction mania, which city TODAY
invests in water treatment to prevent dying rivers? Perhaps one in Europe !

Hadrian's Wall, a Roman-designed border wall to Scotland,
a joke, 117 kilometers long, lies in the middle of England,
in dry peat bogs, rotting when water accumulates,
disappearing in preservation.

The Danevirke Wall, a Viking-designed border wall
to northern Germany, a joke, 15 meters long, the rest of it
lies by the side of the road in dry sand, far from the old days, the pubs rot,
the parts of the wall that are lost during the tourist boom.

Once the accordion has been opened, it should never be able to close again! It is like the numerous opportunities in life to tackle something, to say something, to admit regret about your own mistakes, to even ask for forgiveness.

If you instead keep all these moments to yourself without consent, you will not pass the test of having always acted correctly! It does not depend on the things you have done, but much more on not letting the coffee get cold and taking significant actions, not letting the undone actions lie around, which may make you seem grown-up, but having lived past them until you have the chance to make up for it all is a waste of time! A short life is wasted. The saying still applies: "If someone has done bad things to you, never approach them again in your life!" because it is far too much trust to simply assume that others will treat you with dignity and honesty, or reciprocate what you feel in the same way. When you met them, they were only reflected in your ability to love, but the same did not come from them.

I look at them, the ones that happen outside, the woman as a fat woman, left me standing on her bike, that her figure is not that of a lady, not even that of a woman, her figure is more like the imitation of a male figure, perhaps of her father, or they walk ashamed at the side of a man who, despite her contempt for the woman of her own self, always takes her by the hand like a father, the massive contempt of a woman who always remained a little girl, and even this form shows no movement of her hips that says she has ever really lived out her desires or learned something from life.

Every day that passes becomes a realization for you, which I can see for myself here far away. No matter how much you serve some people and how much you sacrifice for them, do not expect gratitude from them... and no matter what you do for them, one day it will be worth nothing in their eyes. Sometimes you are selfish and give them the rest first. No matter what you do for them, you miss them, even if there is fire and light in you, and if you build hills for them, over the hills of love... you are still wrong. If you spend your life doing this, they will inevitably shock you.

This is how some people are, no matter what you do, you will remain humanly negligent towards them. There are people, no matter what you do for them, for them your actions remain a point on the sidelines. Such a person one day denies your favor and kindness as if you had done nothing, and when he regains his strength, you find that he is ungrateful for everything and stays away from you, and accuse them of being negligent because their most important interests are over and they want more from you without acknowledging what you did before. They needed you and when they got up and recovered, they hated everything you did. But we say: Praise be to God who has implanted mercy in us. He has made us a reason to help those who need us, our origins and humanity, which is no longer present in most people.

They see their own mistakes as mountains that are difficult to carry. Stay away from them, because no matter Whatever you do, you will not reach an agreement with them.

My advice is always be cynical. That way you will never be disappointed. That saying "That in Europe it is mainstream, that those parents and people in many ways abuse their children !"meant otherwise us Mothers saying, "That give birth to children, is still Not - the invention - of those Mother and Child abusers !"

It should be admitted that the intolerable imposition that America's natives are subjected to by immigrants like Trump... that he should have refrained from doing this earlier, at the beginning of the wave of emigration, by taking a cruise to the West. It would have had far less serious consequences. And today, born here in Kaiserslautern, today's Little America City, he would be of no use for anything else and would be playing groundskeeper for the football club!!! If the Crusaders had never existed, we would all have been spared !

My friend, the hero. First he pretended to be Helene Fischer!
My friend, look at him especially since he was playing
the role of Sponshbob today and threw me out of bed with a neigh!
My friend, you're kidding, then he plays the role of the drunk mother
who insults me so much that I'm lying in the corner depressed !
My friend, you've got it that's why I'd better not look
in the mirror in your presence, who knows what will happen next?

I think that strange men on the networks,
all of them actually just comparatively
like fakes or bot characters, act towards women like fare dodgers,.....
they all live in their own little BUBBLE,
never able to escape from it, and I always just watch
how long their job as a "fare dodger" will last !

Do you wanna know how the pimp is in mind ? A strange day.
Life can sometimes play tricks on a man. He wanders among his peers for
far too long in search of love, even before he remembers who he is. It's like
he's living a double life, playing the role of the well-adjusted, loyal family
man on the one hand, and in the other life with someone else, trying to
fulfill himself, playing his second role in parallel, always there for everyone
at the same time, but far removed from the one who lives inside him.

Everything that goes on around him is information from the left, just as
much information from the right, and the poor man can't tell the difference
between the fact that most of the statements that reach him are always more
or less based on the truth of one side or the other. That's why men often
come to the realization, even at a young age, that the severed head of a
lizard could definitely grow back, like its tail, maybe even one of its arms
and legs, just because someone somewhere in this universe said that.

So it happens that one day this man finds himself in a situation that is almost
hopeless, and fate once again awakens in him the revival of his view of the
world, which is his experience in connection with reality.

How everything fits together. It seems to him like a hammer blow from Thor, and the wise insight to understand his life!

He is exposed as a fare dodger. His method of getting to know random, friendly women is to tell them witty stories, to flatter them, to gain their favor, to trust and desire for them directly, to give them tasteless compliments, to act like a fundamental moral thinker, to start from his own helpless situation, and suddenly to juggle with high numbers again, as if there was no other way and not that he was the one who "paid" the women. But until he can successfully "take the fish off the hook" and "soften up" the woman for his own amusement, he throws her a few philosophical morsels now and again to cover up his actual personal hardness, strength and coldness. To make an impression, in repeated devaluations still remorsefully asking for help on how he should behave better in her eyes?
So that the old woman can feel important again.
But actually admitting that he sends his mother into the kitchen herself, who is allowed to prepare his meals every day, prefers to sleep during the day and roam around at night and stay awake, just like a leaf in the wind, until the leaf lies on the ground afterwards and becomes earth again, for someone like him, relationships with people are like mayflies that last as long as the sun shines in the sky, but will fade away again when the weather turns bad. Making a baby for a woman, but first soaking her in a test tube of his feelings, the chemistry of their relationship being more like that of a Neanderthal, giving his sister the cold shoulder, accusing his neighbor of leaving him alone, fooling intellectual women into believing that they are just about adorable for their age, setting priorities differently when women imagine they find a friend in him, not granting the woman wisdom, denying that she probably has no maternal connection to life because her mother has never repented and therefore never seen a real light dawn on her in her entire existence, and in the form of her dog she did not recognize the presence of her ancestors. He devalues the woman's dog. In his opinion, it is always the look from the wall of an owl, like the eyes of his mother watching over him, that he does not commit himself seriously to a woman, as the only remaining son who does not leave her.

That is why the attractive woman has been degraded to him by him to be a sick pussy. The wolf he wants to be, the lion he pretends to be, in reality the lapdog he is for his mother. His deepest wish and desire is to use social networks to take other impressive women and mothers into his confidence in order to teach them about someone else's life and thereby take away their pride, because this is his game, as it is so superficial and anonymous in this swamp of dating, no one can stop misogynistic men from behaving deceitfully and harming others.

My advice is to always be cynical. That way you will never be disappointed. We can't stop the waves, but we can learn to swim. This life teaches patience, not every day is wonderful... and our lives are not always what we want. This is life... it carries many fates within it.
A dream comes true... and a dream stumbles.
A meeting without a date... and a separation without a reason...
Neither the beginnings you expect... nor the endings we want
And life goes on...

Patience for me is staying alive on the edge.
The unexpected happens when you make strangers into friends.
What we know is what others want.
What others want is not good for them.
A meeting without a date may be someone else's moment of enlightenment.
A dream only comes true when you stop stumbling.
The stumbling dream is like an upside-down cigarette
in front of the camper van, and calling this a vacation,
which is recognizable after absolute loneliness nonsense.
Life has a back as long as a dog's. And in the end it's always his cock.

How many people have we lost in our lives because we were too real and honest in all the things we offered?

We have lost because we were unable to fake our feelings and embellish the way we dealt with them.

We were unable to be sincere and open. We do not know how to twist ourselves or take on a character that contradicts our personality. We do not know hypocrisy, politeness and resistance to our beliefs and principles.

We have lost because we have not offered anything except from our depths, because we only care about being ourselves. We have lost a lot, but we have gained ourselves, and that is the most important gain in our lives.

But what happens when people are constantly searching and are worn out in drought, and when they pray for rain, are they never safe from the storm?

If life were simple, the band would live next door to us, our best friend would live above us, the manager would live in the house next door, behind a simple wall, there would be three snack bars on every street, and there would be a view of the other city where you only like duck if you take a weekend trip there. The cities would all be located by the sea. And the breast of desire would be like the salt of the air.

I let my father live his life as he sees fit. He doesn't have long anymore anyway. To deny an old man an evening like this would be a crime, and it could also be that I was the person in his life on whom he acted out his sadism. As an old man, all he has left today is a pitiful legacy of the handful of shabby people around him who put up with him because they themselves don't care about life any more than their noses. I know that in about ten years almost all of those he calls his generation of accomplices, who supported a criminal, will no longer be here. Then there will be no one left of the entire family that I knew. I have already made real inner peace. They will have no more than one last ugly thought, and then they will be no more.

It is said that an Italian artist painted his painting and considered it the most beautiful of all... Therefore, he wanted to challenge everyone with it, so he placed it in a public place and wrote the following sentence over it: ((Whoever sees a defect, even a very simple one, should put a red sign over it)).

117

When he returned in the evening, he found that it was distorted, with red signs here and there indicating a defect, so that the original painting was completely obscured by the red circles. He went to his teacher and decided to stop drawing because his drawings were so bad. The teacher told him to just change the sentence, and he drew the same painting and placed it in the same place, but he painted colors and a brush and wrote under it the following sentence:

(Whoever sees a defect, even a very simple one, should take up the pen and quill and fix it.)) Until the evening, no one approached the painting, so he left it for days and no one approached it. The teacher said to him: - Son, have you seen? Many people see the fault in everything... but the fixers are rare...

Dear reader !
This is the state of people in our world today!! Our shameful reality is that we only see faults, we love to criticize and belittle this and that, but no one offers solutions... and this is due to a lack of love. We do not love each other and do not wish for anything well and success, so never be one of those.. May God bless your time with happiness.

As if it weren't one mistake after another that we have to see, as if our human life was a painting in which each of its mistakes is highlighted in red and then suddenly falls off the wall? But who could endure being alone within these four walls and following this long corridor through all its corridors until they find it, their self? And how can anyone today still endure sending out this self in their head or heart or chest as a pleasant feeling that can be detected at rest?
No more critics, no more morals, no more egoists who are important to everyone! I know the way in which people on the run seek help locked in train carriages, get no water, breathe no air, spend too long inside, let families die in them! Even politicians use refugees to increase the pressure on others, we don't board trains these days that transport people to camps, it happens on land, on water, in the air! Humanity today is worth nothing!

Yay, what kind of motley group of people are you traveling with now? Is it worth asking, or has someone annoyed you recently? What experience can you tell us about someone who is going on a trip...? What languages have you been speaking recently? Can you afford the tobacco, what you like to drink? Will we see each other again this year? If the number of strangers who are assholes is as high as that of our German neighbors, how do you deal with it? I guess you'll move. Do the nights still get long in the beautiful summer? Now that cold days alternate with warm ones all year round, do you still love swimming outside? With all your skills, being such a language talent and being studied scientist, you're a survival pro, it's a shame that I didn't get to do that like you did. I've always wanted to visit North Africa myself, even as a woman. But as we know, it's dangerous for inexperienced men, too, in your continent. So I travel in my imagination like I always do in life. There is still plenty of room for travel, and I will never grow up because I don't give a damn about adults.....

blessings, Heike !

Drinking in the afternoon,
while other people go to work,
then you go to bed in the morning,
then you can start all over again,
in the West they have a stick up their ass,
the little man's sunshine,
are fucking and being drunk,
affirming life in epidemics,
alcohol you evil spirit,
you threw my dad down the drain,
now you want me, get out of here !
Can it be vegan sausage?
Go ask over there on the other meadow.
There could be more victims like you,
it comes as it comes, good luck, you sausage !

We've just run out of meat.
And we'll have to pound a schnitzel onto a vegan roast first.
A joke like "Punch the Lukas" is not wanted,
you can also send him to his death with "stroking".
If you can't stand a joke, you don't like to admit that everyone has disliked
each other at some point, that they were great at bullying each other,
that criticism of everything is the usual way of ruining things for others,
complaining in itself is like the bacterial culture in fried sauerkraut,
that you only keep yelling at others as long as you do,
because it will only make you feel better,
that everyone understands, people are good at that,
because the suffering of others is good for you,
whoever dishes things out still feels himself, he is alive,
and determines what is human only for himself,
so whoever wants something, whatever it is, can pull you over.

The wolf asit on the floor in awareness of the light. That dog aside enters the
room as his mother apologize. The dog asks the Wolf "Who are you ?"
the Wolf answered "I am the friend of the Lion !" - Heike Thieme -

Always be careful of the tempting distance. Travelling alone in Africa
would mean not only being attacked with brutality, but also getting to know
the dangerous animals and standing in a vast field, often without water in an
emergency. These three things in the south are life-threatening, which can
happen if no emergency help arrives by chance. In the north, wilderness is
always romantically considered to be the adventure option, which is also
underestimated, because staying in the wilderness is associated with the
same risks that people usually overestimate themselves for beforehand,
because they always want to do it "alone" as heroes. I'm telling you, even in
the Californian desert, in Arizona itself, people go to the dogs as refugees,
so to proudly talk about all the great experiences you've had out in the open
is a bit overly vain in my opinion, you can just clap your mountain bike next
to the refugees with a bottle of water under your arm and tell everyone
afterwards what you can do!

So why not ride your bike to Iraq, Tibet, Ethiopia or Afghanistan and back, being fed by all the locals along the way, squeezing into their houses and feeling like a hero, and maybe even having your photo taken in good spirits alongside the convoys of refugees all over the world, squeezing past and getting help out of every stupid situation you find yourself in as a paying tourist?

It is not always the distance that matters, but also how far one has learned to experience oneself in silence and to endure the shock of this self-knowledge without judging it. Have fun, I don't want to spoil it for you. I only had my uncle Ernst, the one from Berlin, he used to travel all over the world on his own. And he told me terrible things about Africa. Of course he never agreed with this civilization either, but more from the point of view that the indigenous people and the animal world are dying out. He has been living with his sister for a long time in their adopted home of Copenhagen. They can't even stand the Germans anymore. That's why I say yes, I got to know the family from all sides of the world, north, south, east and west, but I, the only person who had to go through everything, was not liked or welcomed by any of these related families, or could have claimed to expect help from them. That's why I, like you, always prefer people from far away. Best wishes, and take good care of yourself, I would love to see you again in one piece!
I feel the same way. But I also think highly of the indigenous people, who today still live in caves in Africa like in the Stone Age. They really do know everything about us humans. And that's why, when I reach certain personal maturity levels, I dream of these people who praise me for my insight, the women of the high council. They are simply everywhere, but not many people notice them today. People reduce their brain mass, they change their physical constitution with environmental toxins, they misjudge reality for what it is. For so long, they are stuck in a dream bubble that is guaranteed not to save them from any situation in case of danger, but they don't know that. I won't let myself be dragged into any more mulchy church, I'm just not responsive to such slips of the tongue and seduction. It always had a stale, unpleasant aftertaste to have to deal with people like that, NO THANKS!

So that you can hear it from me again, I LOVE YOU, just the way you are!
The indigenous are living their thoughts and the 'civilised' are trying to
figure out their big secrets to profit on, it must always be the big mystery
and complication otherwise all our science and technology has to be a hoax
if you really can live without it...like having all facts and numbers about the
date, otherwise it won't be 'the ultimate match', but that produced mass of
technologized wording chaos, won't bring them further.
This is only the idea of it. But one single seemingly idea that is not concrete,
it a full fupp at the end of the day.

Written by the poet Ahmed Matar*
The story of a donkey, the son of a donkey, is very beautiful

Once upon a time there was a group of donkeys in one of the Arab stables.
One day a donkey went on a hunger strike for some time. His body became
weak, his ears drooped, and his body almost fell to the ground from
weakness. The donkey father noticed that his son's condition was getting
worse day by day. He wanted him to understand the reason for this.
He came to him alone to examine his increasingly deteriorating mental and
health condition. He said to him: What's wrong with you, my son ?
I brought you the best varieties of barley... and you still refuse to eat...Tell
me, what's wrong with you ? Why are you doing this to yourself ?
Was someone bothering you ?

The donkey's son raised his head and turned to his father:
Yes, father... they are people...
The donkey father was amazed and said to his little son:
What is wrong with people, my son?
He said to him: They make fun of us donkeys.
The father said: How is that?
The son said: "Don't you see that every time someone commits a shameful
act, they say to him: 'You donkey...'

And whenever one of their children commits a vice, they say to him: 'You donkey.' Are we really like that? They describe their idiots as donkeys... and that is not how we are, father...
We work tirelessly. We understand and understand. Then the donkey father was confused and did not know how to answer his little one's questions while he was in this bad state. But he quickly moved his ears left and right, then he began to converse with his son, trying to convince him according to the logic of donkeys. Look, my son, they are a group of people, God created them and preferred them over all other creatures, but they did a lot of harm to themselves before offending us, the donkeys.

*See for example. In all your life, have you seen a donkey stealing his brother's money?? Have you heard of this?

*Have you seen a donkey torturing other donkeys for no other reason than because they were weaker than him or because he didn't like what they said?

Have you seen a racist donkey treating other donkeys with racism in terms of color, gender and language?

Have you heard of the summit of donkeys who don't know why they have gathered?

Have you ever heard that American donkeys are planning to kill Arab donkeys!! To get barley?

Have you seen a donkey who is an agent of a foreign country and conspired against the donkeys of his country?

Have you seen a donkey separated from his family for sectarian reasons?

Of course, in the world of donkeys, you have never heard of such human crimes!! But do people know the wisdom of their creation and act well according to it?

Therefore, my son, I ask you to control your donkey mind. I ask you to hold up my head and your mother's head. And you remain, as I promised you, *a donkey, son of a donkey*,,

And let them, my son, say what they want. *It is enough for us to be proud that we are donkeys*
We do not lie
We do not kill
We do not steal
We do not gossip
Do not swear
We do not dance for joy as long as there are wounded, dead among us,,

The son was impressed by these words, so he got up and began to devour the barley and said: "Yes, I will remain as you promised me, father.. I will continue to be proud that I am a *donkey, son of a donkey* Then I will be dust and will not go into the fire whose fuel is people and stones.

Young people of today, such "upstarts", am I not alone in asking myself, why are you standing here in a suit that you don't even fit into?
You are young at heart, where would you actually be if not travelling through India with a backpack? Is that how you want to prepare me for what life without work is like? I know, yes, there are certain things that none of us can see, but that will come our way anyway, without us knowing about them beforehand. So two young men in ties wanted to impress upon me the "truth," that they knew how things could be better in the future?

We scan the circle, what, as a university graduate and pop hairstyle?
With regard to our weaker members of the group,
those with difficult childhoods,
those with an abandoned life partnership,
those with a place to sleep in the car as an escape in the crisis,
how does the financial world react to this in the test?

Have we all brains of Birds ? Because most of us humans, want to live without relationship, and fear that so much to stay single the whole damn life ?

Isn't that funny? I trust you more like an older, mature, wise man, a well-educated, wise man, whom I never knew for long, whom I haven't known for as long as you guys, younger friends I've been chatting with for six years! I suppose the word "older" annoys you, so I'll explain to you that in my way of dealing with people, almost every deep conversation with exceptions was with younger men, who I initially found sweet and nice, but all of them are having a lot of fun, pretending to be more amazing, experienced, artistic, passionate, well-traveled and cosmopolitan, but when things turn out, every time it turns out that they know nothing, don't get to know people who are not well or who really need help, and in these cases they don't even recognize others outside themselves as needy. 90% of people are show-offs and profiteers, people with pretenses who make crude and unfair jokes about others, ignore them and can be quite cruel. That's why I really and truly associate the word "older" with a wonderful quality of people who communicate and write from a real background for what they say - a much nicer and more honest quality compared to the people who want to be the "eternal savages" but who, when you approach them, immediately slam the door in your face so hard that you see stars until you no longer feel the blood in your veins, who themselves have been "celebrated" with their sympathy for years. You wouldn't believe how many times I've seen the stars, probably as many times as you can count the stars in the sky, as if I should behave like those bio-aunts, the absolute oddballs, of Germans, with an abbreviation of all these variable conversations, and still only get laughter that at some point becomes unreal. I know what I learned was to confront myself in all directions and turns.

"A heart that wants and a mind that refuses, and a thousand battles in a body."

There is an eternal battle between mind and heart.
The human soul is perceived only by the Creator.
Do not test each other on this.
The conflict between mind and heart.
A battle that tires the soul.
Between a heart that wants and a mind that refuses.
A certain heart and mind tell it that they are illusions.
Between this and that, the soul is lost.
A heart that wants to fly away and a mind that captivates it.
A heart lost in dreams, a mind that awakens it, and a soul that cries for help.
A battle in which you are the only loser.

If the mind wins this battle, the heart dominates the soul, so dreams come to
you in spectra that the heart desires, and when you wake up, you find that
the mind laughs, the heart cries, and the soul is lost.
And everything in between.

THEY CALL IT.... THE SMALL SECTS ARE GETTING A LITTLE TIME
INTO IT, IN THE STATE OF "SLEEPY HOLZBEIN" or "SCHLESWIG-
HOLSTEIN" it sounded like STARTING A NEW EXPERIMENT, it's been
going on for 35 YEARS!

Does the couple want to show how couples live together, then demonstrate
to the audience, for a bit of piousness, make a group of "needy people" who
are sent to them by the state work for free in a prayerful way, i.e. undergo a
tiny little test to see how well they can be integrated into such "camps", the
couple earn a good bit of money on the side, intimidate the critics and those
around them and witnesses, who report this to the state, and then snoop on
them a bit, talk the children out of it by reporting it to the authorities, i.e.
cheekily denounce them for the criticism, and the newly born child is
"GONE" so that the dear church can have peace again, and a lid on it,
because no one dares to leave the church without the kick in the butt, into
unemployment, which would be inevitable?
 THE REST GOES WITH THE MOTTO – NITIFIATION!

Die Magie der Märchen umsetzen fast unmöglich daran gesehen,
wie die Frauen in der Liebe scheitern,
die Lampe mit dem Inhalt ihrer Wünsche,
die an Ungleichheit und Desillusion scheitert,
Zittern lassen einen nicht die Träume,
es zittern der Frauen Ängste in den Nächten,
jeder hat Träume im eigenen Leben,
die sich unterscheiden wie 1000 und eine Nacht,
es gehen keine solche Leute einzusperren,
weil ihre Köpfe überschwellen schier platzen,
sich laut Verstand und Herz sich streiten, bis sich die Seele Freiheit schafft,
und sie erst erlöst sind, wenn sie ihr Recht zu erst auf deren eigenen Träume
zu zugehen, die Sehnsucht erst mal auf einen Baum hoch jagen,
um sich den Traum dann wie den Apfel mit beiden Händen runter pflücken !
The magic of fairy tales is almost impossible to implement, as can be seen
in how women fail in love, the lamp with the content of their wishes fails
because of inequality and disillusionment. It is not dreams that make you
tremble, it is women's fears that make you tremble at night. Everyone has
dreams in their own life that are as different as 1001 nights. It is not possible
to lock people like that up because their heads are swelling and almost
bursting, their minds and hearts argue loudly until their souls create
freedom, and they are only released when they exercise their right to first
pursue their own dreams, to first chase their longing up a tree, and then pick
the dream off with both hands like an apple !

Watering too late won't save the tree, hahaha, that could be true! I see so
many trees running around each other, and I've been friends with them for
30 years, but they all doubt my integrity, so maybe they all had something
genuine for me just once, but then turned away from me forever in disgust,
and I see them age much earlier, to their detriment. See - life also has its
amusing side! hahaha and when I was a child, no one planted a tree in my
memory, but I created a small animal cemetery for lost and found items of
this kind, nobody could make me fear horses, because the more often they
threw me in the mud, the more often I got up afterwards.

Each time there was no pain involved ! Even as a child I saw that an old man had to grow up before me his whole life like an old turned, carved, dark piece of wood on which he leans, and yet does his work until he drops, and he never says a word about it !
One of them, the little one, was told early on: "Your mother didn't give a damn about you!" but it was clearly a planned child removal and the psychopath got his way. Another one, her child was the means: "You see how... my child is committing suicide! I'll tell everyone how godless they all are!" but it was staged, to instigate the church's susceptibility to racism. One of them learned at the age of 2 to recognize the philosopher in herself that her silence lasted 50 years. "She should be considered insane, negligent, irresponsible and ungrateful!" but today, with almost five years of professional experience as a philosopher, I say: "I'm curious now, father, what will you have to tell me when you break your silence after 50 years!"

The music has to play in the rain,
then the operetta can throw people
with bags of money onto the stage in a bathing suit,
so that its advertising revenue makes an impression,
the cover is overrun by the crowd,
the others should fight the floods,
for an hour of storm surge with concert noise,
just brings in a quick buck,
this also brings the ex-student
with a short event played in the rain
even more for just fake style, and no political statement,
recognizable as "political correctness"
for 50,000 fans, a good 13 million in the ladies' purse.
Dress Men, hostesse service manager, muscles in suit,
serious proposal advertisor, event hall welcomes,
some call it for the callgirls'
Insider tip for organized rapists in the quarry field, next to the lake,
on the edge of the bank, on the gravel stone, for professionals who are
above things like marriage....

We spend our lives looking for the keys to enter people who have no doors.
If the door to a person is only through his one eye,
which welcomed you as well as you admirably accept it,
then all you have to do is smile happily, one compliment turns to another!
Women don't fall in love like we do, my friend.
Women fall in love with money, power and influence.
I have never seen a woman in my life who was proud of her man because he
is loyal and honest or because he cares for her!
How many times have I looked at the one-eyed man?
How many times has he run away from me?
How many times has he honestly never liked me,
and yet always wants to be loved again?
How many names you bear as a man, that's what matters. How many
women you know, man, that's how you approach me.
How many times have I tried with you,
and then picked myself back together in small pieces.
What does that have to do with money and gold?

In contrast to supposedly my big emotional problems,
which is why my child was stolen from me in bed with violence...hahahah,
I am an experienced horse groomer, was a prospective geriatric nurse,
had training as a physiotherapist, my knowledge to support the disabled,
created good artistic paintings, conveyed my social skills and knowledge,
well, and as planned, I successfully
raised my child to be a self-confident, clear-headed person!
No matter now, I didn't become a missionary victim after all....
how this kind of mission is translated
can be discovered in any cemetery at any time !

After the fall of the wall, nobody cared at all, try it out,
it tastes light, like strawberry & chocolate, the chosen model child,
never has to work, the bastard child, just has to slip up,
its anger drove it to flee, until then it was persecuted by him,
even a bungler needs "pride" in life, he tells the story for the rest of his life !

It always goes so far, to be rejected by your father,
who only meets you with the flat of his hand in the face,
who considered me to be "his mistake",
who never felt like a daughter, but did everything to have a real "father",
Everything who locked me away for years,
called me insane, for the violence that was done to me,
Everything he tried to do, let me rot there,
NONE of it. NOTHING can be made right again!!
He was just waiting for the day to come
when he would take my child away from me and...
for the day to come when I "PUNISHED" MYSELF!!
I don't fly straight into someone's arms
when it comes to love, I don't need a quartet!

I'D RATHER MIGRATE TO A NEW PLANET!
TOMORROW THE WEATHER IS SUPPOSED TO BE BETTER AGAIN!

Passers-by who are quick to communicate...
I should approach them in a healthy way,
I should show everyone else scepticism,
I should take an example from them,
I should tell the graduates their motto,
I should get out of their way,
I should not get on anyone's nerves,
I should ask my ancestors what they tell me,
I should not approach them a second time,
I should fuck everyone to the moon and back,
I should show respect to the professionally trained teacher,
I should always show my smile,
I should never doubt, not even myself,
I should translate their regret as guilt,
I should interpret their rejection as unfortunately
not being able to make it in time,
I should pretend to be unconditionally interested in them,

I should stand with them in the middle of the rain,
I should act like a fool for the sake of the officials,
I should come crawling for love,
I should pretend to be a country girl,
I should block out their perverse desires,
I should first be abused, then serve in friendship,
I should always greet the little haters,
I should send little messages to stupidity,
I should enthusiastically call their descendants geniuses.

Had just finished the new book, but haven't got the money to publish, then waiting until next month, shall go and make that new title and the new cover, that makes fun, it is silently said, really my life essence in describing the psychopath in my father, and inside of another story, my essence, then the consequence to me and fazit to learn of it. It is wonderful spoken, if it was not ME who has lived that Life, then nobody would have found my PHILOSOPHER in me ! one of the ones i wrote who are good advisors:

against the young girls fairy prince syndrom i wrote...
"Direction to future days", against the women marriage complexity i wrote "Ask the jelly fish", against the abusive politic for ex. in USA i wrote a solidarity book "Loyality" dedicated to someone in OHIO, one next english version shows short cutted the image to bear the worst in stay positive, to carry life along in a positive way, like i do, still no title, against the abuse in online proposals, to make aggressive business on good believers with lies and fraud, i wrote the book "Careful with the Dating trap "
but my books got more, ...then now i have got 122 books !

The most won't pay with money anymore, the lesser work, the books dissappear, but the lesser also will read, they misluck in the thought to be wise, because they have not learned to criticize, and have not taught themselves to handle self critic, they are dreamy babies then, manipulated by a machine, maybe IF trump will raise, this will be their first and last Big Baby fart in USA. They will then leave the rest world in chaos and war.

131

Who cares, who just made a business thing out of it, have you heard it ? that coward wants to raise all taxes to every single product entering USA from outside 200%, stupid cow i would call that idiot, he has too much honey milk in his brain, but none who milks his sick brain !

If you get no respect, but epileptics in crash helmets
are allowed to act authoritatively towards you.
If you are unmarried and are the scapegoat,
not the competent employee, and you are denied a wage yourself.
If they want to be chaste, stay at home, but send their husband,
for a low-value feeling, to ruin your reputation. If paths goes downhill,
drive you away, chase you to the churchyard, serve you contempt in the
morning, their personal sorrow at lunchtime, serve you a toast in the
evening, ALL THEIR YES-IN people you have enjoyed German culture!
Everyone is against you, turn around and you will become the leader.

I assume that the man is almost impossible to save !
He looks like an American, with a deep erotic voice,
alone in the fitness center like a piece of meat in the display !
It looks like the hysterical stalkers, the supposed future mothers,
the wallflowers sent by dad, all spend their lives waiting on the dung heap,
for someone to finally free them, were sent there for him!
I only advise him, "Don't make yourself part of the potato salad !"
You will bitterly regret it ! With whom are priests... in the best hands?

They like to be freed, from their addiction to sex,
they feel under pressure, they always have it on,
how many times a day do they do it, they get it on,
perhaps with professional ladies, in hiding in the house of worship,
to cast off their shame, to talk openly about their obsessions,
with a woman who knows her body,
who knows it like Santa Claus,
after all, they all want to be freed !

Firstly, daughter doesn't take drugs.
Secondly, daughter doesn't know jealousy.
Thirdly, daughter doesn't bring father a bastard into the marriage.
Fourthly, daughter doesn't stop at nothing.
Fifthly, daughter has no plans of her own,
the patriarch goes to a sex therapist, he cheats on her,
the daughter scares off every suitor, then, as someone who came too late,
with his money, the new apartment, as a gift with concessions,
the desire for grandchildren, or even two !

Someone told me, "If you were obedient to the king, you wouldn't live in a
hut." I told him, "If you knew how to live in a but, you wouldn't have
obeyed the king."

What is fitting for a king? What are young people today?
I'll tell you... it is not important to them
that life is only earned through work,
that life is about human aspects,
that the old people showed them how it was
who learned that working their backs off is normal,
who know it openly even in old age, work
that can give in gratitude for life,
like children today can no longer say thank you,
like the joy of mothers for growing life,
how it is all the same to them to face life,
where young people look at their mothers from behind,
with the rear end first and step out,
with the awareness of guide dogs,
with ignorance strive after kings who pretend to be blind to the grown
flowers that are their mothers, recieve their love, and fuck them off.

What is attractive to you in a potential partner?
He might have known a lot about those women he had,
and cares with honesty about it.

He could give answers of experience, about matters of me is interested,,
and shows an interest in get to know me.
He learned to care for the garden, house
all about children matters, and knows about the worth of life.
He taught himself to share about matters of friends,
and gives himself as human, and not as a king !
THAT IS ALL HUMAN, what i want.

EMBARRASSING A father who gives up his house,
advertises his company called "broken", his house, the child finds out,
lives in the shadows, no one outside notices, the little one at his side,
has his father-in-law, look after his garden like a servant,
because anyone who is stupid enough to
give up an inheritance that is actually too early,
doesn't have to look after the flowers, he should just do that himself !
So you see the little old woman standing there,
with her big bush, and all that is visible to everyone outside is the roof,
that's how it should be..... huhhhh.

Where there is no king, there is no suffering,
where there is no half-measure, there is no ignorance,
where there is no arrogance, there is no self-righteousness,
where there is no remorse, there is no solidarity.

THE "WAY" of creating POVERTY!
Planning child expropriations in advance, before the child is born,
using violence, bringing together the traumatized,
subjecting them to stigma and persecution, stalking and bullying,
proselytizing, discriminating, then suppressing them
for a good twenty years and keeping them "unemployed" by force,
statistically suppressed, inciting hatred, a mother-child breach,
there is sometimes a huge gap
between "legal" and "humane",
Mr. X !

We know the existing Nazi law in the country.

Like my brains say "I only repeat back that body is right handed; I'm not all plants and animals in a paradox of everything = nothing" :) .... try this in another language, reading left to right (handedness): the future in general, including dreams and night and day dreams, is perfectly vague as it belongs to all future pointers: 1+1 = 2 specific, coordinated points: #handedness = #now = #forever= "physical ± bodies ± connected" , "the end" of what movie is "the only end for every other one",

so the role of imagination is to imagine a healthier planet for all observers, including younger plants and animals = evolution = ethical preferences #life = #like (vs suicide and murder, for instance, as sacrificing children to the sun or some wack shit adult cultural pathology), simply observe that being physical intelligences is now "neither alive (created) nor dead (destroyed)".

handedness means I can't speak for another one, I can only hope physics and biology go viral: we will always have (at least) I+I biological parents, each.

I hope human adults will stop thinking we're all other plants and animals combined into some paradoxically (false) virtue-signaling abuse children's 1+1 =2 physical brain sides: "zero origin dollars = carpe diem = zero end" You are true. Thank you. I do not often find solidarity, but i am always in life that one telling the truth, as much lesser is the consequence that peopl try to listen to me. That Way People have to become big Artist one day, because you cannot build a node in Brain and prove them not to think, this will be a next english book from me...

I know every single bone in me. I feel each one of those veins bring me oxygen. I am shaking my thought with empathy and soul and music in speech. I will never give up my physically and will ever love more the way than the end of the road. Not to paint, sad but true but bring out to the puclic all this, causes much confrontation and pains, to go through, but you recieve many more insights with it, i know what you mean, but all people have the own movies to dream, i see some people may be sooo far.

As well as they are the same brain triggering and have same humors, that they are so fucking close again, we all come solidary to the similar brains easy as well as we all had once or twice the same aim at the end of the road, but had still to walk and a walk so long, that we started to enjoy the long walk more than the end of the ways, sometimes the Buddha is found in yourself, like you do too.

Yes, sometimes a dream image in the morning first was superflous or funny to see, but at the following day this was the essence of the daily teaching, like you said it, then you have reached the point to be arrived at nature, today was a raven from the top of a house downtown he spoke and sang to us the publicum, this was overwhelming.
I am a writer, physiotherapist, artist, geriatric nurse, experienced in working with the disabled, ... I believe I would have been a good mother to my son, who was born on 11 August 1997 in the maternity ward in Kiel, and was hushed up, that I was denounced as pregnant, that my child was forcibly taken away from me immediately after birth, that lawyers made me aware that an old Nazi law was in effect, that declared every child removal "legal" without justification, that a lawyer had no authority, that my son was still abused in front of my eyes, and even then passed on from foster home to foster home, that when I got my son back, he had already told me about his abusive experiences in the shower when he was 2 years old.

ABROAD the church does this brazenly, it illegally expropriates newborns, sells them for forced adoption, declares them dead to their mothers, collects its money in all possible "areas" for this.... TO EACH OWNER HIS OWN WAY! And just like i remembered those aquaintances of real people from Italy, here or everywhere, they are steadily liars at me, that one who confronted me very sudden with his dick pics, the one who forbid me the mouth as german musician and hippy in Italy, the other one who told me not to contact him directly Mr. Wilde the other musician, and the last who tried to carry me to church in his massive brain watering .... so tell yer, that Italian language won't be my interest, reading with translation sometimes but nothing else, i am not the one Deer for the italian hunters !

It is impossible to missionate me !
At the time of "Franco" and "Hitler" in western Europe it was said
"A woman must be married. A woman must have children.
A woman must obey her husband. A woman must not vote."
Their western European dictatorship therefore resorted to stealing babies
from women and selling them to the highest bidder without children.
This has continued to this day, all over Europe children are stolen, sold and
abused, as a lasting legacy from the time of the dictatorship, because the
laws allow it! Not a single lawyer has any objections to this.

Would I sit with another woman around a hole
in the freezing snow on the frozen river while fishing in the cold,
to "hang" him in there for a bit? Asking her the question "Did one go in?
Then just get him out again?" and looking at the fat roast, she looks down
and says, "No, I'll let him squirm a bit longer..."
has it ever occurred to a woman to act so stupidly?

If I, as a philosopher, learn how I, as a daughter, fuck my mother, then I was
told I needed a psychologist, if I, as a philosopher, see how my surroundings
fuck children, then these neighbors are called pedophiles, then I consider
everything together, like me, unemployment, maybe God too, and my soul,
and everything around it, in that I only concern myself with myself, being
banned from working, and consequently only knowing myself, but the
whole world doesn't care about sin, and God doesn't watch anyone
masturbate, and they still rub themselves against children today. That's why
most people think they're God, and want to be left undisturbed in their
activities. This year's child is added, "CHOSEN", which is normal, and
afterwards everyone is always disappointed, because they are much more
DISAPPOINTED with themselves !

I imagine how I would see it as a man myself if women came to me early,
whom I didn't even want to know, I would whiz away from them like an
arrow, preferably by bicycle to the edges of the world, to find freedom in the
wilderness, I would always be up and away so quickly that these wooers of

137

youth and marriage-mad Stone Ages, who would grow old early, and their dreams would end with me under the waterfall, in a sight that was supposed to be the same, like a herd of men only with long hair, and I meanwhile always stand on the edge of what they are doing, as a climbing flower reaching for the sun, I would become a vine, a slender one, and the women would become fat men who get their men married, that they would feed the women, reproduce, eat, drink, reproduce, maybe get rich, not much different from the animal world, except that animals don't humiliate, even if they eat each other!

I prefer to look those who are selling me friendship in the eye. Helps against nasty surprises! No, my skills with strangers are exhausted. The sooner they tease me, make me look stupid, and contact me now and again, reject me and then approach me again, is not what I want, so I am increasingly distancing myself from the games that concern me. I said at the beginning that I have no intention of forming a real relationship with strangers online. And I no longer trust the whole thing. Who knows, maybe you will find someone else who you can pressure into marrying you. I am not available! I no longer have the will to take in tourists, actually no one at all. So I'm not doing it ! I've explained to people that I've realized for about half a year now that I'm incapable of being in a relationship, and I realize that I don't want to and can't have a partner by my side because it just doesn't work for me.

WHAT IS IT A SURPRISE TO ONE...THAT THERE ARE NO PROFESSIONAL OPPORTUNITIES FOR DEDICATED WORK WITH THE CHURCH, or PERMANENT EMPLOYMENT? The Pope is just as unselfish as all those who work for him. The Church lets normal, well-working employees with a humanitarian standard spend years slaving away for contracts, blackmailing the chronically ill with false promises and church double standards for the doubly suffering workforce, ruining careers by requiring medication, but by ratting out others, postponing the risk of being fired, and by allowing workers to have a say, immediately terminating the contract for continued employment.

My theory of "the big bang until now" is short, we just spoke about of our theory what was first, the egg or the chicken, then i told them shortsaid my version, and the both had many things to complain, was funny, at least we closed that all in the world wether they are muslim, christian or viking, nature believers or even living in an african cave, and on island they all do believe in the right way they want to, and all things to believe in a better future for their region they live in, and none is better than another not the region nor the people with their believe, one friend's wonderful saying and wording from the Koran made me happy very much. Those both kids, brothers are the kids of the single parent father. It feels good having that understanding between, not many think it over, so that everyone may speak and talk with everyone.

1. was the tree
2. was the worm eat the apple from the tree
3. was the worm lay eggs
4. was the worm becoming a snake
5. the snake grew to a raptile
6. the raptile got wings and flew
7. while the fish in the sea climbed on earth
8. the new land citizan got a fur and four legs
9. later on the mammal was also calles human
so my theory is first was the egg, then was the chicken !

"Would you like to sit at the right hand of the Lord in paradise, bathing in His grace and ecstatically enjoying eternal life?" "No."
Hypocrisy! They may hypocritically protect churches to save them from decay, they may depopulate the countryside, the farmers may go bankrupt and move to the cities, they ensure a careful image of preserving the "old", but on the contrary, as with everything that ages, there is usually nothing left but sand and stones, because where would the church be if it were about displaced persons, asylum seekers and the poor rural population, about wanderers and lonely travelers, if no one was living there anymore anyway? but what room ? i find the most old buildings now are rotten.

So how would the Pteridactyl want ever stay inside with us ?

Women who work in bars are women who "open doors" for rich guys,
I'm not one of them. Women who stick to their bars are women who make
promises to men, "keep the door open until..." the money runs out.
Men who fail in marriage are always honored by women
who make it easy for them, that's why they're called... "easy girls,"
I'm not one of them. Men who have people working for them
whose only skill and talent is to throw their dignity to the dogs are not good.

Nature whispers sweet nothings in the ears of its beloved earthlings. "See,
your child's future fades in the wake of your escapades. Pay heed, let earth
flourish nature is to nurture & cherish or humanity will surely perish."

Charity bread! Death of thought! YES, you can twist and turn it however
you like, there is always a catch! If Nazis are remembered in the memory of
their children as they see them... as if they were individual body parts, next
to each other in test tubes, neatly arranged on the shelves, not labeled with
their names, NEVER, but neatly numbered, as they did with the J.... back
then, do YOU still know the pretty blue and white striped sheets that the
disabled, Jewish children, orphans and unwanted people slept in? their
children then think that they should not have become so forgetful, how else
could one forgive the old people when they no longer understand, because
they confuse forgetfulness with mercy! Who has realized? Who doesn't like
to admit that they don't like to admit anything at all? Who doesn't blame
others first for the fact that their life is so shitty? Who doesn't see
themselves first, but in a better light than reality? Who doesn't know that the
numbers on their negative account and the years of failure are plentiful?
Who hasn't seen that you don't just get more beautiful as you get older?
Who needs three beers before they become brave? Who only lifts the
mountain in their minds because work is something others can do? Who
only looks others in the eye when they think they have a cowardly mob
behind them? Who cries out like they're crying out for their mother's breast
when they don't get any recognition?

A Race like a Wolve !

Memories in the head are like broken glass.
The more our thoughts move, the more it hurts us. One young woman is seeing red often these days and it's not because of her favorite color- she's been chosen by the goddesses of ancient Rome to be the last keeper of the eternal flame. It's going to be one hell of an assignment for someone who never knew the Vestal Virgins even existed ! When you look back and realize that you don't want to go back, you know you're on the right path.

When they are invited to a coffee alone on the deserted beach in the morning, when they see the fireflies and just hold their breath,
when they remember the double shot they had with the elf on the edge of town, when they are still just sitting there, the smooth, huge full moon in front of them, which almost swallows you up at the sight,
when they are reborn in the cold water, when they remain fresh and alive, like a little fish in the water again and again, what more could there be, would it otherwise be like a net that scoops you out of the herring??

Unsterblichkeit ! When a girl falls from the sky,
then empathy for her only arises if she was still whimpering on impact,
because she was a celebrity, that one mourns, her past fame,
it was supposed to be her jackpot of the evening,
and ended in a fall from a great height. If a girl from a normal background
was the one who fell, and was like the apple of her eye,
her death would never lift her up into immortality !

Girls in obscurity. Girls in the isolated role of the Internet.
They all die as number zero, and they are not even mentioned for the shame,
the disgrace and deprivation they suffered before of any kind of suicide !

Dignity and her long shadow ! A man has his worries,
will he survive, will he not, walks on two legs, lives and loves whoever,
until he feels he has to bear his weight, as every human being should,
until his gaze follows the path, like a long sip of beer,
to be tied down is never really his wish,
he lives with the wind, he does not tie himself down,
his love is in the universe and applies to everyone,
his intention is doubtful until the day breaks,
he never wanted to stay in one place for long,
and said, only on the day when he looks at the sun,
and the face of a laughing woman in it,
who recognizes him by the fact
that he does not cast a shadow,
who wants nothing from him,
who will not buy anything from him,
who will not take anything from him,
who does not want to "MARRY" him!

Good morning, dear sunshine !
Share the good mood and go out and in !

Now I know what I've learned from social networks, especially Twitter, that the standard has sunk so low that it's mainly all the guys who are far away who only act with fictitious CVs, who confuse all women with a herring swimming around in swarms, who you just have to pull into the boat like a fisherman with a net, with the "marriage" and a thousand stupid sayings, until every sensible woman repeatedly realizes that the person she's talking to has no shadows at all! I'd better go shopping quickly and get a few things from the store, that sounds more realistic to me.

Everyone needs to know "THERE IS NO FREE TIME FOR GANGSTERS!" I don't care about: your appearance - your family - your skin color - your age - your position - or your money. I care about: your personality, your mentality, your morals, and your conscience, and on this basis I will respect you.

If your brother betrays you, you have two options.. Either you kill him and regret it for the rest of your life, or you forgive him and spend the rest of your life with a traitorous brother.. If your brother betrays you, you are defeated in any case. I know if he studied the whole life, how to surpress his sister, he playes the mouth organ, and farted to his ceiling,
while watch his sister naked come along even with a belly,
and a shameful face of a coward, he believes in his desillusion
to be told a succesfull person, doing all the best.

If your brother betrays you, you have two options. Either you kill him and regret it for the rest of your life, or you forgive him and spend the rest of your life with a treacherous brother. If your brother betrays you, you are defeated in any case... I know that if he has studied all his life how to suppress his sister, he will play the harmonica and fart to the ceiling while he watching her come naked, even with a belly, and a disgrace in the face of a coward, he believes in his disillusionment when he is told that he is a successful person who is doing his best.

Can you tell a German man by when he plugged in the
new dishwasher yesterday?
Does everything run smoothly for him if the washing machine is within
reach because it was only replaced the day before yesterday?
Does he perhaps have better chances
with his wife if the coffee machine with pods is the latest thing?
Are erotic moments for the bourgeois
when he is out and about as a financier a combustion engine?
Do all the women's eyes follow him when the very latest dryer is plugged
in in the bright white basement?
Does it affect his flatulence if he doesn't know anything about Thermomix?
I today just had looked outside my kitchen window, while the next roof
outside sat both ravens, as loving couple cuddling and kissing each other
and were very proud me witnessing this love.

People always said "Be warned, that Microsoft has pretty many technical
breakdowns !" but what about those men, with the misogyn behaviour and
really bad style abuse womens rights ? What is his mind, is he fleeing ? has
he killed someone and runs, is he witnessing a life long traumatizing crime ?
has he a brain defect, his eyes behind a mask ? Perhaps a severe headache,
there is pain in the image, he really tries to escape. His hair a helmet,
sometimes the figure of hair dresses are like hats and mask and modern
style, to make none look behind the veil. I remember those youngsters and
guys in my puberty, they had very seldom anything to tell, but heads filled
with drug and alcohol and dirty dance, stupidity hidden behind a strong trees
stump, and those girls all do philosophy about what adventure is hidden in
those "hearts".

Silly girls philosophy, he is sleeping under that tree where he dreams of his
love climbing up there, and it is only him alone who went to bring her
down, and no other would dare to climb that tree where the lions sleeps,
young girls dreams might be, i never had it like that. It it is reality, jou let
the young ones be in love, real life is lurking around the corner early
enough, i am heated by the weather here, rainy and wetness in the air.

144

Like a djungel, this is enough in thick air, this is even the fight with the dragon until you get up. My good old dog, she is labrador, she is strong. But there are few ones, i met such a lady, she spoke of her suffering dog, with a fur as thick as ten centimeters stuck black long hair, she said today, when he laid on the road exhausted in the shadow, that she shaves his fur twice a year, my theory is that the often shave made his fur grow even stronger, that poor dog is at the end, you see it, the more you shave the more growth, poor creature, uhhhah i think they would send me to hell, if i did that to my dog. I only knew about that one lady with her dog he is white, long hairy naturally, and she takes his white fur to knit whool pullovers with it, no when she gets the hair i think she does comb it carefully out of his hair, combing is better, it is work but the fur for knitting is practical and wonderful, yes, it frees the fur from heat, but the hair grows still slowly. I think usually that nature does make a change between winter and summer fur, but that poor lamed upheated dog with the fast growing hair now, i think he will suffer until he gives up his hell and dies.

I see those people also might do those faults in raising the own kids, they do give the kids tons and tons of chemicals for each sneeze, cough and fever, uhhh. I learned and know to give babies a chance to live, and be born, meant the knowledge to give life, that meant, to be responsible in what you bear in your both mother's hands, to give the good medicine and instinctual right thing by time, every mother shall know about it, not a single usual male doctor will ever have interest in what is the best for others child, not more than the mother ! But their kids never play in ground and dirt, so they will never touch an animal, and will not recieve the natural immunity against deseases, those suffer then life long allergy. This is unnatural, i say, let them stay asit in the shitty pants, but never let them run in a meadow naked and explain to go for little toilet alone, fucking people who will later on not recieve a thanks for this. Their kids develop to be the "winners" and the seemingly "loosers", those who are winners, let the other clean their asses, like a slave, and those loosers, stay in their shit and do not learn of it, it is a degenerative life where kids grow. Never questioning the order of things, the upper ones never come down a step, and the under live in the ground

145

and eat the dirt. And learning to kick downwards, while the upper one does not learn human skills, he has no ability for empathy, and is out of reality how cruel he is, while the under living in the ground might have the chance to behave social and climp up in the society, the upper one dreams of a kings life, while lying in his shit he produces, while the poor one thinks okay, that he will never choose a kings life, because that king deserved no respect.

But i say, every empath lives and survives by that thought of hope, watch them pass with biting dog and unkind face mask, and the young child in the waggon, i am laughing tears but with the rest of power like a wheeping almost sleeping tired horse from the race.

One day I asked a wise man:
Describe to me the device...?

He said: Having happy or sad news and not finding a single person to share it with.

I said: And exile?

He said: Being in the crowd while your heart and mind are elsewhere.

I said: And silence?

He said: Appearing silently despite the relentless noise in your head.

I said: And maturity?

He said: Deciding what suits your mind regardless of your heart's desire.

I said: And strength?

He said: "Appearing steadfast before people while having a great wreck in your heart."

I said: What is harder than waiting?

He said: Losing passion for all things.

I said: What is harder than sadness?

He said: Getting used to it as if it were an integral part of you.

I said: Describe to me the pain?
He said: When the letters are different, the word hope turns into pain...

I know you're right. I also feel sadness as the driving force to keep going,
the same driving force as anger. I know that for me every time I go outside I
have to prove that to them, to be steadfast. There is no other way.
I stood and felt empathy, that's what makes me who I am, and every person
outside who I meet with questions makes my fate easier.
A twin girl happily and demonstratively showed me her "deflowering" and
came back to me with tears in her eyes. I looked her straight into her eyes
one last time as I said goodbye. A small fish in the crowd can still swim up
and away. A woman who has run all her life can still stand patiently in one
place and wait for what comes. Silence is only unbearable for young people,
but their thoughts return to calm when mature people from both sides take
them under their wing and tell them something about respect. Maturity is
only noticeable when you talk to people who feel understood by you, who
feel that you accept their distance, giving them the time they want for your
invitation. Strength is like being locked in a narrow corridor, but absolutely
having to get to the sun. In fact, more difficult than patience is accepting
yourself, letting go, and finding the bridge to yourself. Even more difficult
than sadness is the inability to act.

I would not be suitable to act as a tourist on Italy's beaches, I would then
feel like a fish and coral-eating worm with spikes on my body and would
injure the local children's feet, and why should I really be interested in
taking pictures in space with some kind of probe, flying to the moon in a

rocket, and babbling about the physics that gets spaceships there? Even today, the invention of the wheel, like back then, has not earned any convincing recognition, except that the human population had overpopulated the whole world like a cancer.

Jews, these people are known to be violent and highly aggressive in their way, but they have never achieved control over all people, I experience this here on the streets too, Jews proudly introduce themselves to me with their first names and broad smiles, and soon wish I never spoke to them again, and certainly not to be called by name in the city. They only ever have violence in their consciousness, you know, narcissistic people also have the ability to verbally put themselves in the spotlight at all times and in all places, simply because they cannot feel the human side, the empathetic side. What is happening in Israel is really recognizable as narcissism. Immeasurable tragedies are taking place, but a narcissist who is responsible for all of this looks on, it does not touch his heart in any way, but to put himself in the spotlight and to remain known as a leader, it is just a clumsy attempt to be in the spotlight, ... otherwise, according to his own courts, he would have been sitting in a prison cell for a long time. This is so pathetic in human terms that you can't even comment on it out of disgust and the sight of it. I really hope that these boys and girls, mothers and fathers who are dying in a hail of hatred in a mad rush manage to escape at all costs.

I don't think much of Jewish plans and I don't think much of such theories, for me there is no beginning of the end. It's a dance among people, either they hold each other's hand to protect each other, or the traitors among them will fare badly.

Don't worry, if a narcissist continues to approach me with some absurd remark or conspiracy, scaremongering or piety just for the simple fact of willingly offering their own child for lynching, in order to get absolution from me, to get praise for betraying their own child, I always just tell them the unwanted truth to their face, EVERYONE!

Narcissists are lonely creatures, inhuman narcissists who only know THEMSELVES. As a woman, I simply stand by women, it's natural, and when such degenerate behavior is nurtured and acted out towards their own children, I declare such women to be "sick people" who will never know. They have not dug a tunnel to convert the world, but simply never left their prison cell on a tiny little North Sea island again because their guilt will never let them go.

It's a desperately sad image. A kid, maybe 13/14 wearing military garb too big for him. Clutching his rations tin in the hope (presumably) of finding some food, somewhere.

It's the narcist Mom of that kid,
she was willing to manipulate
with a weird mind, to press the child
in that suit to fight the Mother's war,
she has sacrificed her footspring,
wanting to press the public for that
like missionate the people, by force,
destroys the child, and wanting
the attention for her, as a hero's Mom,
she earns just One single place,
to stay where she once came from,
the tiny tipsy Island in the North Sea,
and stay there alone in her prison Cell !

How to stop the warmongers making profit out of war. Tricky.
Yes, that is like the poor dog, digging and digging so long for profit, then stuck in the own hole, and people have to get him by his tail.

This is the story of the strange man on the street, completely according to my version, it is currently being put online by the publisher. "Yerba Santa". Today I had a vague idea of the second story I am working on, the story of the girl who grows up in the barren, desert landscape in the country with her family. It will soon become a book too. It's as if you could think of ten books a day. But then there will soon be 1000 books, including the English ones, and no one is reading them. I haven't had a holiday for ten years, or fifteen? And before that... twenty-five years ago.

How do you live on the street? You dream very hard, everything is so close, even the one bed you once had, people are either lots of them very close or few who stay with you, you always get lice from the animal world which is annoying, the people, even those who can stand being close to you, don't talk to you. The night alone, hope far away, hunger, no goal, no home, but then a full moon as big and round as the sky that makes you forget everything. You only sleep in a sleeping bag, if at all, or in a narrow dark junk room, or a bunk in a women's hotel for three days, small travelers are often needed for work, but the overnight stay is not always pleasant, if you travel as a woman you are so thin that you don't have your period, you don't even think about it anymore. It was laughable once when I wanted to get back from Spain in a hurry, annoyed by the lice and so thin that my jeans were practically sliding off my hips, then I asked a friend for 10 marks and went to my grandma to wash the crap off my head, ACCCCH honestly it's amazingly relaxing to finally be able to walk without lice again, but I'm sure if I had asked my grandma what it was like back then with no money and starving, she would have told me something similar. Today, children are taken to school and back by shuttle, even to kindergarten, tssss, my son almost always managed the journey alone. Even a very lovely, slightly handicapped man walked almost the same route through this town to his workshop in the morning, so I simply asked Nansi from the fishing village to accompany my son to his school for a bit while it was still dark in the morning.

We live in a time of complaints, we have never had it better,
but everyone is offended to the point of extreme zeal,
the zealot of the time, who sees everyone who thinks and acts differently, everyone who looks different, everyone who seems strange, as a reason for complaint. that "HE" still sees himself as a "VICTIM" here...

It is the German way the zeal - the hysteria. So people are always happy to take jobs abroad because... less bureaucracy ! I matured with the pain that no one taught me how to overcome, and I grew more than I should have when I faced situations that I never imagined I could overcome...

Mothers who lack empathy.
Marriages with such people do not share anything with the outside world. They do not like uninvited guests. They do not want the psychological crap to get out. The anger is in the consciousness, the victim's knowledge. They are angry spouses but also cooperative, because they have no idea what those who know are capable of. They play rhetorical skills and think, maybe in retirement it's a matter of letting the other person win, and staying polite and pretending to be forgetful. They would no longer trust anyone who experienced abuse from their daughter within the family, if this meant that their conscience was always armed with weapons. Anyone who says nothing for a long time and hesitates acts fascinated. They counted the seconds in which the daughter, declared by him to be insane, healed countless wounds, processed the unspeakable, first in a long film without text, until she escapes, just as every single day of her childhood outside had been an escape from the family.

The patriarch's only interest in talking to everyone is to find out where this feeling of shame is generated? The human brain consists of various modules that work closely together, but also have specific functions. Take this painful feeling of shame and self-loathing that torments the father because he wanted to whisper suspicions and things to his daughter that never happened. The father confesses: "Where is this feeling of shame generated? In the anterior cingulate gyrus and the parahippocam gyrus, both of which belong to the limbic system, a brain structure that is crucially responsible for the emergence of emotions. And this structure is noticeably inactive in my wife. That's why I chose this woman. She is the husband's mirror image and a reminder of the abuse he committed against his daughter, like an accomplice. That means she cannot love, pas de chance!"

That's why I can now understand people well in all their depths and abysses!
Now I feel better that I finally found out the secre t!

Morality and double standards - Where human rights are ignored !
Consequences of brutality the image of the black person in the world
with a view of every city whose own character shapes the image
the photo shoot of the image machine the life itself of people
after social exclusion and expulsion, the highest poetry lies
in the unspectacular view of the moment.

Some of us are like ink and others like paper. If it weren't for the blackness
of some of us, the white would be deaf, and if it weren't for the whiteness of
some of us, the blackness would be blind.

Love paid its prize. Girls like her are cut from a different cloth.
She wasn't made to sit pretty and keep her mouth shut.
Girls like her complain whole life.
She wants to be in everyones thought.
She is missing the importance role.
She has not the style of a gentleman.
She is disgusted of children in her size.
Her boobs make it all wet. The money maker is the hero.
Her boredom is paid with dollars. She is the laziest mom ever.
She stood first for her prince. She fell latest for his hate.
She never worked at all. Girls like her don't earn Mother and Father.

"We live in a world where funerals are more important than the deceased,
marriage is more important than love, looks are more important than the
soul. We live in a culture of packaging that despises content."
- Sir Anthony Hopkins -

If I see this husband who went the wrong way
disregards, disrespects and fools with my marriage as such,
i would not dare anything better to say G'bye
and he would still marry the next, then confront her after wedding
with fraud, criminalty, cheat, distrust, shame, sploit,
he could even rape a woman outside, but would return as husband,
into her bed each night pfui bahhh ain't really really not worth it,
until people then started to laugh.

I wouldn't date a man if there was even a hint that he'd find doing this
funny or acceptable. Sometimes that means you end up dating very serious
men who don't joke around much, but this is thoroughly undignified and
embarrassing to your respective families.

This is also why when girls tell me a top thing they look for in a man is that
he's funny (not a sense of humor, but funny), I have to wonder. A lot of
"funny" guys are just clowns, and it takes more discernment to figure out a
true clown from a lighthearted, funny guy. And it's how you end up with a
clown shoving a whole cake in your face. It's one thing to put a piece of
cake a bit sloppily into someone's mouth. Throwing a whole cake, mashing
cake in someone's face? Clown behavior.
My friend and daughter in the neighborhood would of course have a lot of
fun if I still wrote things like I did ten years ago, for children and ordinary
readers, but I have developed a lot further. She made me a special present, a
bracelet braided with four leather straps with a silver clasp, which she gave
me as a gift just as she was passing by. My dog is blown away by the two of
them, she just throws herself down in the grass at the daughter's feet and just
wants to kiss, cuddle and caress her, my girl and I, we are also experiencing
such overwhelming sympathy for the first time, and we are happy to return
it! Such coincidences happen again and again....! I am not the ageing, lonely,
typical German eco-aunt who just waits in her dolly apartment for someone
to come knocking down her door for coffee and cake, and I don't need to
make such offers anymore because I'm slowly getting to know normal
people who try to spend their time as usefully as possible for themselves.

My new theory is:

I believe that it is the South, this globe, created by man, that serves to create a world for men, to live there independently of the influences of women, to turn away from society and its politics in old age, preferably with cats and dogs, and to simply enjoy being old on the beach and in the sand along the shore with a bit of music and peace. So I will be careful, now that I am starting to get older, to squeeze my whole personality into someone's life. Because I no longer think I am that important. And the time to duplicate myself in a child-friendly way in front of the eyes of the man of my dreams has really been over for five years now. You said that a tree that is watered too late is probably no longer able to grow, no matter how much watering is done. I say that a woman whose garden she missed all her life, spending time there with a loving man, is probably only left with a wild garden where butterflies fly freely, and she is simply a guest in it.

I see that the tree grows without my doing anything, and I have never given up seeing the beauty of nature. Whoever you are out there.
Thank you for your poetry !

Someone approaches a depressing situation
with intelligence and a sharp mind and distinguishes between two things - what is said and what is done. The perpetrator of the Nazi era experiences a narcissistic insult in his own memory ! It's the uncomfortable thing that probably damages his self esteem.

Give your child a lifetime of joy. As a mother, I speak of the true purpose of always being honest with children, even if the truth can be uncomfortable, you will see, it will fill you with external effectiveness.

TO EVERY ANIMAL HIS PLEASURE ! You have no idea how many unpleasant interviews I have had to endure in eight years, all I can say is, my friend, keep your health, your love always means pain, no matter who you are dealing with and on what level, I confronted myself to the core!

What is beyond the window, though?
Speechlessness fainting Moms who bear the abuse of kids
who bear the own abuse, who bear the violence from the State.

"I'm telling you, these are people who now describe their lives to me, even as adults, uhah. Do you know that the toughest guys from Algeria say that it is well known that Europe is best known for the fact that almost all of its children are abused? I'm telling you, these are people who deeply regret what we are going through here, who have to live and endure in the most restrictive, spy-monitored, unfree systems themselves, we feel sorry for them." It makes your ears flap.

In the last few years, including around 8 or more really intensive international interviews, I have done a lot of creative work, which has helped me regain my mental health and balance, I have painted, written and even given a one-off reading in March. Last year and this year, I have written a series of books to explain my relationship with men in life, about marriage, the dating madness on the internet, the misogynistic attitude of dangerous men, the resulting terrible social consequences that women suffer from not going under, and, thirdly, my treatise on breaking away from a family whose father was a sadist and whose mother was an unsympathetic accomplice. Mentally, everything is perfectly fine with me, a Russian neurologist has just confirmed this to me directly, he has also examined me. I am far more fine than my family might think, but I don't care.

Yes, life is an up and down, I always feel very sorry when I meet people online who do not miss the opportunity to hit on me, but always with an insult in the compliment, and an attempt to deliberately fool me, which I can easily see through, and a way of offering to be best friends, until one day I am only meant to sink into shame for them because of their ulterior motives. Then they always feel sorry because it always ends extremely painfully for them when they see through it, with them realizing that they have irrevocably fallen from grace with me. They then present it as a "love disappointment", the idiots.

But this is also reflected in their own clumsy attempts to humiliate a woman like me, it always ends in the exposure of their intentions, instead of me falling apart like a house of cards. It's funny that these guys still confuse this with an "attempt at love", really very pitiful. That's why being on Twitter has become very trivial over the years, it's almost only misogynists and matchmakers around. You get used to not even taking this portal seriously anymore.

It was linked to the first rape, the expulsion from the cold-hearted family, then the second rape while hitchhiking, and the third rape on top of that, because my grandparents just kicked me out. Then, on the advice of my lawyer, I fled as far away as possible, never to come back, on the advice of my good lawyer. Considering that I lived alone in exile in the "north" on my own, the tour continued like this. When I was pregnant, my father denounced me again, and the child was brutally stolen from me in the confinement and abused in the following period until I had the child I wanted again. My little son was so small that he was able to describe to me what had happened. I won't say anything more about it, but when one bad luck happens, it brings countless more in its wake. I am a nursing assistant, a former masseuse and lifeguard, a writer, an artist and have relevant experience in educational work with disabled people. But the church eventually kicked me out of the job because of my "past", as is common practice and widespread there. Despite all the annoyances and a stalker I reported and some other nice neighbors I have come across in life, I was still able to turn pain and loneliness into a happy existence with sufficient awareness, and my son turned out well as a human being. But the early, violent break-up of 1 1/2 years was enough for that, and we were never able to build up our emotional bond with each other again. We now each live completely independently of each other, but we are both pretty intelligent boys, so I never have to worry seriously about Julian, my son.

You can leave it like that, I am no longer staying in the south because of everything that has its roots in my family, just to protect myself, my family would destroy me at any time.

Photo collection from school and childhood. Sorry, that would not have been possible for me. I had no possessions at home. One day, according to my lawyer, I was on the way to being forced to go into hiding from my family, to flee with papers, a backpack, my last salary and a few clothes, plus my little diary, and only later to settle in the far north again via Denmark, or my father would have destroyed me and locked me away, he had sent spies after me and wanted to drag my reputation through the mud, declare me insane or deprive me of my rights. But the lawyer gave me free passage and said, "Now, finally, take to your heels and never come back here. Live your own life as far away as you can! Your father is the devil, but thanks to the latest legislation he had no means of achieving his goals." Well, I had no more than would fit in a shoebox at the beginning, as I said, the "good old days" did not exist for me.

On the subject of LOVE! People dare to do a lot of things.
Hooking on someone, listing sound insulting comments
feeling the kick, announcing cheating, confirming in a benevolent way
feeling the kick setting a trap, being rejected and insulted
acknowledge the false identity, attempting to set someone up, the kick
YES; THE MOST BEAUTIFUL THING ABOUT PEOPLE IS LOVE,
but.... did you always only notice afterwards when the train had left?

Do you always only notice afterwards that you were happy?

Today i got mails from some people of the old school class who want to meet for this year and showed their first real interest in how things are going, they got short said my life things going since that time, and i got an old foto of the class, and those names of us, funny things they told me to have been the most intelligent and pretty girl from the class, but they wish me seriously to stay here where i am, not to be in danger to be closer to my familiar past and all things that happened against me, they want me to have in future good times. I spoke to just one of them, and he won't trash these truths in the group of others, he said his own wife, the second one he has, she had the same rapist trauma until today suffering.

To those patchwork children they have now two small extra bonus kids very young, and they had such an experience of violence too, i mean here in the Exile of north, i never had it like that sameway, that none was interested in my person, until the last days, now there is carefully bit by bit a friendship to a neighbor Mom with daughter growing, and it feels VERY NEW but awesome, yes, a newer life feeling. But we do see us seldom, then do spontaneously talk or drive to swimming, no plans, no termin, no coffee and cake meets, just being free, and she must go to work and raise her beautiful daughter, no private visits, because she has a lot to do. Mable is fully in love with them. She knows all about the work with handicapped, like i do. She is a fairy like me. She knows the same fairy books. She is totally tight and solidary with her kid. She comes from a North sea island being born. She has many things in heart and longing like i do. We know so much of each other, when each one talks, the other knows. She has been lucky as nurse to find a job there, and i was not lucky to enter in such a work, like she knows now. Church is choosing like we all know, the ones who are the winners, the ones who will never be. The ones that church abuses and the ones the church tries to therapy as abused. For me that theme to work for church is OVER. My past is OVER, and i say in sight to my family, they pass and i don't care to have known them, but i know that i go the better way.

Yes, as the same presidure i must work on with the next translation to explain the last project how it was meant, these three books i offered in german.... this was a quick research.
The first book showed the total complete truth behind the veils of psychopath men, and misogynist and the life story following for the women because of this deeds.
The second book showed the consequence of a victim of those sadist behaviours, who stumble through all the traps of society and believes, and life phases.
The third book showed the end of insight in my private life, compared to the fate of a woman with the sadist father and the mother unable for empathy, and his and her roots from where this came from, then how the daughter raised like a phoenix from the ashes. Then follows a novel !

Stupid people would say this was my knowledge, the insight and life's experience, but i say, No ! - the life experience, the knowlegde of violence and the last happy surrender. Surrender being the keyword and what we all need to do to get past any traumas. Surrender to me is finally being tired of being tired and bringing it, or lifting it up to God, surrendering it.

I know He/She is on the journey with me so I don't have to explain every time, but does require me sharing my honest thoughts (that generally opens up more to me!) damn, didn't know I had those thoughts about it too!!!
 When done showing Him my cares, I ask a creative question, how can I see or know this different? What can I do, etc? (never why) and move into forgiveness by deciding I will trust to see and know it different. I always get an answer when I ask and let things go, thus making room in my cup for a different knowing.

I'm sorry that happened to you or anyone else in the world! Happened to me too, not violently, but still messed me up for many years until I got tired.

Hope this helps in some way. P.s. Every experience that we have we file in a good or bad file cabinet in our minds, called our subconscious mind and that subconscious makes up appx 88%. Way to refile is to consciously tackle, find another way to see it, believe it.

Namaste.

It is not easy to say goodbye if you want to stay. In addition, I was afraid of goodbye letters, so the goodbye took place without letters.

Saying goodbye without letters, is like never having been there,
never having reached her heart, is never being heart and heart.
Saying goodbye without letters, like someone else speaking for themselves,
is like trying by force not to hold on to what is best for you.
The regret was for knowing you, not for losing you.

159

Marriage
Knowledge of human nature
Cutting the cord
No Guilt
Own Way
Confront
New Thought
The craftsmen always have a bell in their pocket

'Four years in, 'before' has become almost irrelevant.
We can't afford to think about how things used to be.'

The lights go out at a company,
the boss has been shot,
barely buried, his successor-in-waiting,
wouldn't like to cancel Christmas,
in the interests of the company,
along with a foreign Santa Claus,
he'll accept that, but...
they doesn't want multiculturalism,
the whole spectacle for the people,
to bring the company a little closer to them,
who else stands alone,
who doesn't take care of the advertising,
the fat pink girl at the reception
doesn't want to have to fall off the meat,
just out of "charity"
and for the future of the company,
he won't cancel the celebration!

What isn't enough?

That the woman looks like a fairy-tale princess,
that everything is blooming in the butterfly garden,
that the kitten is fed to her full potential,
that her husband is a handsome young prince,
that the roast rabbit is in the oven with seasoning,
that the house is big and good enough for guests,
that the table is pleasantly set,
that her dress is a little open on the leg,
that her pumps are a cry for her dress,
that she could dance the tango with pride,
that her foreign guests have traveled from far away
that they can taste her roast,... well, will that go well?

The narcissist sees in his face the harmonic,truth,awakefeel,attracting
desires, that he will ever have trouble to reach without any help ! Give me
an army of men and I'll make them all bow. Put in front of me only the one I
have feelings for and I will bend. If one day you get lost and don't know
where to go, you have a place in my heart reserved for you...

TRUE HOSPITALITY CANNOT BE SUCCEEDED BY ANYTHING!
Which one does she put between her legs?
The gardener and the Swatch worth the price of his entire year's salary?
The charmer and the woman on the sofa, and finally the impression
with the harmonica and the sofa cat? The punctual guest sipping rosé,
his wife marveling at her uncomfortable shoes?
The cleaning lady cleaning the stairs in the background,
who still apologizes for everything, for being late,
who does everything even on her birthday?
The hostess of subtle make-up, the guests' faces covered in make-up,
and expectant looks. The lady of the house, with a posing look at her
husband, considering the timing of the roast,
wouldn't she rather ask the guest to go to the toilet?

161

Operating one, two or three buttons just to get an airplane to fly is worthless. If you only follow these controls, you can finally take off. But landing also requires knowing how to land. Most people always take off first, and only once they are in the air do they realise their mistake, that their knowledge was only half-true, and crash.

How else would I have learned physiotherapy if I had not experienced first-hand how important adjustment is, that is, vitally important? How could I have learned about having children if I had not witnessed a child in a woman's womb until it was born? How could I not have decided against this profession if I had not examined real corpses in anatomy? How could I learn to distinguish that natural medicine is far superior to all scientific medicine if I am not a friend of animals and people? How would music be recognised as such if someone has not played for eight years and four-handed in the presence of a teacher? Why study people who know nothing about life and death?

So relying on half-knowledge from books is like marrying the wrong man in the belief that you know nothing about him and just telling yourself, "it will all work out..."?

The best part of you will not appear in the mirror because the best part of you cannot be seen by the eye.

I am aware, thanxx for your words to be bond to many animals,
I am a creature of nature, to answer them and get my news,
I am a flower that no one cut, to let me blossom everywhere,
I am a part of the ground i came, to be strong like the grass,
the best part of the heart is felt, with erruptive emotion
is cried out and laughed out loud, this is ALL !

The king has no friends, only followers and enemies. Happiness is not a goal, but a journey that we live in the details of the days. This is heaven. I agree.

Give the one you love wings to fly freely, roots to stay, and reasons to come back. Leave some space between you and the one you love, and don't be so concerned that you suffocate. No matter how beautiful a cage is, it doesn't change a bird's longing for freedom.

I need none believer missionate me
sorry then i think we are on the wrong adress
and i am not serving any God, my whole family did not turn
to a religious person, so do i, people who make their own believe powerful
you better not make the people afraid like that

I can say goodbye, but I still don't know how to leave. The married man thinks the single man is happy, and the single man thinks the married man is happy. So who is happy?

Perhaps it is the man who seeks shelter in the branches of a particular tree
so that he may notice a vault on its trunk that looks
like a ball, which he takes, and holds to his stomach,
and falls into a deep sleep with it.

Anyone who shows no respect to the young woman in my presence,
but threatens her with nasty sex, even in front of her parents,
must be told like a mama's boy how to behave in public,
how to humbly apologize, how to insert his finger into his own penis,
how to swallow the condom himself in front of others!
That is the right language for them !

Anyone who cowardly takes it upon himself from a safe distance to a
woman who is resting in the sun, pointing at her with his long arm
outstretched and laughing loudly, will hear from me that there is only
one thing for him, the basketball club of a team to meet the right father,
big and broad, who doesn't even fit under the door, not even in width,
and who still has to teach someone like that what respect is!

Anyone who stands in the water to witness a new student taking a
swimming course and laughs loudly at them as a man for their attempts
during the course deserves nothing other than to have the hard block thrown
from the bank with a loud warning right in front of the frontal cortex, and
that from the daughter's mother, without mercy, without mercy, even if the
stick misses the mark in a long throw, she will throw a second one after it.

Anyone who only expresses themselves politically in order
to be seen as a rural fuck machine, who trivializes atrocities in politics,
that sees dying people as bycatch, that sees destructive warmongers,
that sees future-destroying activities as useful,
that shows the conspicuous stupidity of belonging to the eternal yesterday,
that still declares the Corona epidemic as non-existent today,
and still demonstrates against it today,
that is, compares the chance of advancement in the provinces
with the upstarts from the piglet factory,
that only fathered children in order to stand out in the crowd,
and shout loudly for Trump, and praise the apples at the market,
that gets a trip from me as the dumbest young fish!
That sign is about one guy held himself for Daddy's best one, and forgot
about the sign warning not stumble over your feet !

Anyone who strives for chaos, and worships the wrong god,
so wages war on innocent individuals in schoolyards,
who does not protect any of these victims,
who accepts deaths, whose father pays for their school career,
whose polo shirt and hood stand out from the normal school uniform,
who obtains their certificates by deception, buys them,
and gets them as a gift from the A-grade teacher without an exam,
who wants to be considered a future generation,
to claim sponsorship for free studies, and today still has to laugh
mercilessly at the victims, remains in the human race, a hypocrite
who is to be pitied forever, and is no longer taken seriously
by the parents of victims, and witnesses of this!

When a septuplet with seven sisters realizes that all the other seven, like themselves, succumb to their own thoughts and never remain the same, go their own way and in doing so love other people, we know that there is no one truth! I would not want to meet my seven doppelgangers in the same place, at the same time !

Women have let me down here for twenty years.
I helped myself, I am at peace with myself.
I made my own peace within myself.
No wonder they are all crawling to me now,
trying to condition me with all cheap means.
You can't condition me.
Because I don't even BOW before an army -
but before the one man, because I recognize
that I feel something for him,
at most all I need is good friends,
or the instinct to know that there might be
certain people who stand behind me, who I meet.

They look at the audience, they live by being or doing,
they can do nothing, they regularly look at their mobile phones,
they only see their reflection in the mirror, some kind of captured face,
that does not speak to them, that does not express itself directly and clearly,
whose facial expressions are not legible in speech,
whose inner stability in knowledge is missing,
that they know their subject well, they imagine that they are not educated,
and do not want to work at all, but hold out their hands,
quickly through fast Internet fraud,
trick their own company into submission,
and only readable in the small print,
they deliberately cheat and lie to their customers,
because whoever admits that they are the better ones,
grew up in the cry of the breeding piglets, with a lot of sibling shouting,
but above all else, to say what a good stable they came from.

AMERICAN "Win Win" is your DEAL,
so just a BUSINESS in which the KNOW-IT-ALL profits.
I ONLY ADVISE ONE THING IN THIS CASE - BLOCK!
and DO NOT CONTACT THEM AGAIN !

I know these providers,
who first go to sound out the sticking points of all those,
who start up their thinking apparatus, and let them fall cold,
then appear in a different look, and offer themselves
as a Christian promise of healing, actually first scold people for being open,
but then want to resolve the traumas with people,
sell themselves as altruistic and non-commercial,
only in your case, but not otherwise,
don't want to give advice on the false trail,
don't talk honestly about facts, but show a smiling picture and...
they themselves only suggest, out of human hobby,
as a win-win situation in a continuous loop,
helping people in the name of God,
so they gain all the people's "knowledge" for free,
and in gratitude the people are "helped" to submit to their faith...

Corporal punishment, people! Do you honestly believe that
it has been abolished because it is prohibited by law?

Psychopaths who beat little people who have children, do everything that is
possible on the helpless, small people without a lobby,
and only in their thoughts... so.... that blood flows down the walls,
and no one but the children sees it !
This criminal, bungling type of person has not yet been abolished by law !
That is the whole appeal of believing
something is possible that is only prohibited from the margin.

Never assume that you will meet someone better than the experienced
family gruesome, Go and chase away the prince, better dismount from the
white horse, and you keep the horse for yourself.
Meeting of feelings ! When an ideal met, children wanted to be born,
where one had not planned to meet her,
her, this supporting role of all, as if she had not existed before,
he suddenly wanted to live with her, give the grey its color,
the hearts float heart and heart a life, until they pass it on to their children,
the actors teach children to play, the musicians teach children to go on stage,
the beauties teach children the leading roles,
but if she only tries to live her feelings,
the child says to herself, who did not learn to stand alone,
why did the father have to go before her, who created a uniqueness,
but in the mother's life was not there for anything else?

The main characters in the film are people for the shooting stars it is
completely natural everyone else is ridiculous
the emotionally trained golden children are served by supporting characters
but they also only live in imaginary worlds, they miss nature, its sounds
and feelings, the innocent ones among the winning children
will feel the revolution in its beginning to mean the most important thing
for the future all children without fathers, mothers or history just look
at empty screens they are considered untalented by the shooting stars.

It is unfair to send a naive girl in ignorance of family matters
first and foremost to where she learned how things work.
She has no substance, she knows no ancestors,
they did not follow the road in peace,
she herself did not learn to laugh at the devil,
even without expensive money and jewels.

It is merciless to send a naive girl out to the road,
first and foremost to trust the demimonde,
where she learned how people die from them.
she has no language to reject things, she knows no protector,
those who followed her have no friends.
It is bad theater to think a girl is a pussy,
but to pretend to be the great hero lion who replaces her missing father,
and chases her through hell, as if you were making her into a horse
that everyone is giving a good smack on the butt.

Fine girl... sits at the bus stop at night,
can boast that the young man would do anything for her,
he himself presents her with the sounds for the film of her coming fame,
she doesn't believe in fast sentences, she doesn't trust grey cats at night,
but she talks about being something special,
her assignment is not for a friend, who is on the run from murderers,
but she realizes that now she has sent him away,
and she is sitting at a dummy, and her bus is not coming.

There is no fixed form for man. We are constantly changing... Words,
situations, days change. We are just a reaction to everything that happens to
us. In this life we play the role of the survival of the wolf, the strength of the
lion, the hearty eagle, the song of the whale, the sleeping old bear, the
hunger of the seagull, the hasty fish, the thirst of the mouse, of the bees in
search, of the dog that lives on the street, of the snake that lives in danger.

Stupid men allow themselves to
change the weather themselves, influence the wind,
produce goods for everyone, which nobody needs, which are superfluous,
make poor people work for them, who have no lobby,
search for the fine gentleman who got them into all this trouble, who
stopped their revolution, whose autocracy begins here,
in the factory, and this little girl stands there,
as if she still had the question, where her leading role had gone?

The girls love to trick, stand wet in the rain
believing there are no dry kisses, but then mom comes and delivers
new clothes from the tailor, because love is not in the way,
she screams against every wall in the house
how wonderful life is, in contrast to outside,
where clever children are the most important thing to her!

The old story of the first pigs, they brought the colonizers,
do they want to repeat that today?
Not feasible, when the factory workers are already without pay,
and there is no luxury, nature is going down the drain in the same,
but no one is standing up for its preservation, the poor rich are worried that
no one wants them as slave drivers, that no one is willing to take on the role
of the outtakes for them, and even sells them the goods
that are to be produced that are not in their price range?

They say, "Emotions are all well and good,
but they only apply to your own children",
the win-win situation is that the work you are aiming for is handled
as a kind of self-censorship, you play mentor, within permitted framework,
and you must inevitably learn
"to protect yourself from thoughts that are not permitted!"
that is what they are teaching children
again in schools today with promises of salvation...
They walk in step in the club and learn this and that,
so they drink and eat together, and philosophize until midnight,
in reality they catch people who they thought were preachers of love,
they rip off their skin, they take away their speech,
they imagine that you can change people by taking away their rights?

It is enough honor for them to know that we left them, without betraying
them or treason as they did..!

You know, her work ban and her exclusion,
as tasty as wine from Georgia, awesome, the little housework,
and off to the cozy garden to grill, the unemployed person can wave or say
"hello", is only concerned with her front door keys,
that she always finds her way home, and all her poorly paid work,
doesn't help her with her pension either. Ah, I would go crazy!

A bit of Fit for Life today! Tomorrow the wellness option with sauna.
After that 1/2 hour group meditation. Wired up with all the high earners.
Thursday evening squash. Friday reading fairy tales to adults.
Weekend barbecue with neighbors. Monday chill out again with gymnastics.
Ideals are hard to sell. The men's quotas are higher wages.
Women get 4.5% less than €4.50 per hour. Know! Know! Know!
You can't get a job like that anymore. Those who keep pride stay at home.
Privacy awaits, no betrayal. But no family outing either!

We play a role of the wolve survival, of the lions strength, of the eagles
heartfelt, of the whale singing, of the old bear asleep, of the seagulls hunger,
of the fish in hurry, of the mouse in thirst, of the bees on search, of the dog
live in streets, of the snake live in danger.

A bit of Fit for Life today! Tomorrow the wellness option with sauna.
After that 1/2 hour group meditation. Wired up with all the high earners.
Thursday evening squash. Friday reading fairy tales to adults.
Weekend barbecue with neighbors. Monday chill out again with gymnastics.
Ideals are hard to sell. The men's quotas are higher wages.
Women get 4.5% less than €4.50 per hour. Know! Know! Know!
You can't get a job like that anymore. Those kept their pride stay at home.
Privacy awaits, no betrayal. But no family outing either!

We have been talking for years that our nature is dying out, the population
inland, those who live in isolated areas, in forests, will soon find nothing
there but rubble and flies, maybe a few leeches, maybe 1/3 of the fields,
maybe no more inhabited villages, just a few inns, like in the Middle Ages.

Bands camped around each other and people drove to the farm in carriages,
the ones with the wigs, and entertained people whenever they felt like it.

Little stupid friend, or employee of friends...
it goes like this, you give someone money,
the snowman gets almost all of it,
you get nothing back, you find three more,
they lend you more money, they don't get it all back,
the "profit" goes almost entirely to the snowman,
so "me", you have a small part,
they have to borrow something again,
most of which goes to the snowman,
and they don't get it all back, and so on and so forth,
it's like dealing on the street, that's clever?
You, who invited me to love and then withdrew.
I still don't know what the story is or why.
As if my heart were a doll to play with.
I wish my heart hadn't gone. This game that they're talking about.
Is the trivialization of their shame. Is the slander of their intentions.
Is the silencing of their thoughts. They are the ones who, called by name,
no longer have the courage to greet you!

They teach you everything in life, except how to live without them.
We haven't changed, my friend, but situations have revealed everything to
us. Don't waste yourself building others up, you might be their first victim.

Don't give a damn on the highest tree,
he will have to send you once back, what he stole from you.
Don't shout at the sisters, but be aware to warn them,
like the arrow right between the eyes.
Don't hesitate to teach your children swim,
they might see you as your saviour in life.
Tell those who danced with joy over pain,
that days revolve around their people.

Reminds me to the breast of a female murderer, pretty well grown as tree !
The navel is like a little hole for a little tail to stick out of it,
and the breast is more like a collapsed building,
wart in it the entrance to a cavity, underneath the cave of evil speculation.
A person cowering in front of witnesses, mouth that of a murderer's den.
The posture shrinks to the support. One wonders in front of friends
whether this causes great "suffering"? But the old woman only complains
about the shoulder strain a year ago, the pain must still be horrendous! In the
meantime she can't even connect the term "physiotherapy" with "moving for
therapy", her tendency to let herself go like a sack of potatoes.

His body may be lame, but his brain is genious. Someone who is weaker
than you but smarter than you can save you in the moment of your defeat.
Work with a handicap, work with them with a handicap, and you will know
from the first moment what a good body you are blessed with! Someone
who does not speak to you but feels the entire universe, from the earth to the
moon, and protects you willingly, you will experience him as the one who
protects you, because actions are real even without words.

ORGANIC GERMAN!
I know what you mean first they put him in a cult, then they refuse to think,
drag themselves back to their parents, fall into the same corners,
to hide from work, finally lead him to the labor camps,
there saying "yes" and "amen" to everything, their wings soon clipped,
their aversion, their care broken, can no longer empathize with themselves,
their brains sold advertising, like a scented fabric softener,
out of the window, declaring every man a pawn, selling cheap labor,
to every highest bidder, like every online provider these days,
with a perfidious fraudulent sales concept !

People who talk back...are denounced with high treason !
Anyone who, thanks to a...in short "ideal marketing concept",
"thinks he is the sun", and pushes the Patachon aside, to tell him that
"he is better off with the dead", the bird may still impress teenagers,
but will soon find that the ground beneath his feet
turns red like the floor tiles "Pride often leads to a fall!"
Comparisons can be drawn to semi-sects,
for example the picture of the sea lion and the wooden leg....
for example the picture of the defensive role model....
for example the picture of the seven-fold Cross of Merit...
for example the fashion of the exaggerated defense club...
for example keeping your mouth shut in order to roll off, run away...
for example that women have no place in such fashion clubs,
for example that it is only about prestige, eating pizza
and having a round of beers, example no "little woman" will become a great
ONLY A MAD THING THOUGH THAT WAS FUCKING!

A bad singer may have singing lessons, but no style.
A bad lyricist walks off the stage with a pee in his pants.
A bad boy band wets its pants when its mother's water breaks....

The remaining employee at the school for the disabled is a simple educator,
housewife and mother from the vocational school, who chose the easy way
to get a job, but who did not manage the easy way to work by not looking
for the way on foot. She frowned upon entering the streets of ordinary
people, taking the small street to work, stopping at red lights, admittedly
opportunistically but by entering the rooms of disabled children she smooths
out her everyday working life, representing her mother's half-knowledge for
the church. She acts for a "clean image" to show off her autistic daughter,
and even if she goes to college one day, her mother will ignorantly retire,
and in addition the opportunist's dog simply ran away out of contempt
because all around him is her hypocrisy.

However, people who have real training and experience in life and who also offer guidance to disabled children are deliberately kept out of the professional field by the church and are becoming unemployed on a large scale and are no longer taught anything, even single parents!

That was perhaps a kind of fad 40 years ago, but it had already been over by the 90s, and Germany had already gained a reputation as a poorhouse around the world, and there was no question as to what these widespread "farms" with incapacitated slaves who worked there were for, who were brought to the church in an eco-friendly guise, actually so much for nothing, to hide the fact that the Nordic GOP, in comparison to the way in which the Nazi law systematically arbitrarily disposes of German-born children, including all those with only a small amount of German parentage, in accordance with the North's open decision to dispose of any right to deprive women of their rights, and steals children from women at birth, specifically from mothers who have medical knowledge, intellect and education, as well as mothers who see the child as their desired child, including the use of extreme violence and the slander of the mothers.

Because whatever is possible will be applied within the framework of German law, including laws dating back to the Weimar era, and lawyers openly say that they have no means of stopping it, not the slightest!

This totalitarian approach will not be abolished until, for example, every GOP veteran in America has his weapon taken away from him!

"This constant lying is not aimed at making the people believe a lie, but at ensuring that no one believes anything anymore.
A people that can no longer distinguish between truth and lies cannot distinguish between right and wrong.
And such a people, deprived of the power to think and judge, is, without knowing and willing it, completely subjected to the rule
of lies. With such a people, you can do whatever you want."
~Hannah Arendt, (Oct, 1906 - Dec, 1975) German historian and philosopher

I have known the whole process from the perspective of other mothers for eight years, even Canadian mothers whose only father has German roots were dispossessed by this arbitrary Nazi law from the north of Germany, just because the father had brought their little daughter to German soil. From then on, the father suddenly had such a right to deny her the child and, in an attempt to make her a criminal, to threaten her with imprisonment.

Immediately after the birth of my son and the violent separation, I was locked away on the grounds that I was "too sick and therefore posed a danger to my child", but these people themselves mistreated the child in front of my eyes and he was almost abused in the host family, which my son later described to me in the shower the last time he had contact with these people. As Child you are always fucked with German Blood !
NO GOLDEN KISS and LOVE by FORCE !

When women are often disappointed,
or simply do not have the charisma for eternal love,
because her new man did not even give her "eternal youth",
they run to the disco at night, so that her husband can feel the jealousy,
while she picks up the first guy she sees there among...
overweight, old men and sick people, and uses him for cheating,
she doesn't care either, because she finds out
that he only has about 1/2 year left to live,
unimpressed by this, her husband leaves her anyway,
and afterwards it only damages her reputation like the times before.....

For one it is a burden that she does not have a passionate lover.
For another it is the stupidest chicken that she finds to marry.
For the other it is the journey that is too long for her to find peace
and lay her heart at someone's feet. For the other it is the lie behind the curtain, her sister, who serves as an excuse that she has the absolute freedom to love you forever. They all only love under the pretext of money, and in return they give them your head ! You give them exactly that picture, and they steal it from under your pillow.

175

With the fire of my own soul I am taking my quiet walk
to the Sea of my own salt... But before that, let me wish u happiness of life...
Let's talk about the Capricorn standing in a country where war is raging,
crouching on a small rock, not knowing where the path will lead.

Let's talk about refugees, whose status forces them
to endure so much more suffering, until they feel safe in a foreign region,
until those who stayed at home do not have to suffer serious consequences
because they fled.

Let's talk about nature, where the animal world in the cities
is one of the last to make itself heard in a striking way,
to catch the eye, to highlight itself in a film,
to occupy the satellite to tell the world
that its space and the human space are among those at risk.

A person is not obligated to show you the stress they are going through so
that you will leave them alone. And if you find me by chance, don't run
away because I won't ask you to come back to my life. I want you to see that
I'm still alive and it didn't kill me..... Your separation

PEOPLE CAN, in my opinion, really now,
REGARDLESS of their sexual inclination,
feel the desire that is innate to them
with their own bodies.
Personally, I have had absolutely
NO INTEREST in a relationship,
simply because I experienced beatings
and violence at home, and that can make you lose interest.

A person is not obliged to show you the stress they are going through so that
you leave them alone. And if you happen to find me, don't run away because
I will not ask you to come back into my life. I want you to see that I am still
alive and it did not kill me... Your separation

The patriarch's only interest in talking to anyone is to find out where this feeling of shame is generated? The human brain is made up of different modules that work closely together but also have specific functions. Take the painful feeling of shame and self-loathing that torments the father because he wanted to whisper suspicions and things to his daughter that never happened. The father confesses: "Where is this feeling of shame generated? In the anterior cingulate gyrus and the parahippocam gyrus, both of which belong to the limbic system, a brain structure that is crucially responsible for the emergence of emotions. And this structure is noticeably inactive in my wife. That is why I chose this woman. She is my husband's mirror image and a reminder of the abuse he committed against his daughter, like an accomplice. That means she cannot love, pas de chance!"

Never forgive a person who has hurt you again. It is honor enough for them to know that we left them without betraying them or committing treason like they did..! A person is not obliged to show you the stress they are going through so that you leave them alone.

I think that people can really now
NO MATTER what their sexual inclination is to feel the desire with their own body that is innate to them. I personally have had absolutely NO INTEREST in a relationship so far, simply because I experienced beatings and violence at home, that can make you lose interest.

Who seems to be able to help themselves
by exchanging their alcohol addiction for positive thinking?
Who only matures as a thinker with an alcohol problem
when they realize that they are actually an alcoholic with a thinking problem? This "ALWAYS BEING IN THE FLOW" nonsense.
The damage that is caused is irreparable. How often have the women here tripped over their own feet because they were not prepared to say hello to me for 35 years? Strangers were more likely to recognize me, even after 20 years, from the day they met me.
I recognized strangers by name, even after 20 years,

The constellation,
that only one mother living not far away but at a distance,
the same education and interests, the same single-parent situation,
the same long-term ability to get by on her own,
with a gruff parental home, the drones on their island,
the same experiences with... relationship-related psychopathy,
that only one person has not been impressed and infected by widespread,
usual rejecting exclusion, like an epidemic, common in Germany,
not worth mentioning further, not particularly highlighting,
not of great interest to me.

A HIPPO ran after his daughter, the Doberman, which he sent after her,
the ladle of manure, on which he placed her,
"The tickler" as he called the daughter,
beat her until she ran, for he called her his fawn.
When she escaped he turned white, like the wall, like his skin, like his hair,
like his shame made him red, so from then on he always ran alone in circles
around his trunk, on which the daughter
had knowingly not sought protection.

"Anyone who believes that others are to blame for their own dissatisfaction
also believes that pencils make spelling mistakes!!" © Albert Einstein
He wanted to PREPARE me for REAL LIFE?
No, really, but what do you think, in time
in the foyer of the Old School, after a few years in prison
with the worst murderers, on the mountain of knights,
in front of all the staring eyes maybe UNHANG me without WORDS?

It is time for rapists to lose their courage,
the little secret of the student from Zeitler's class,
wall to wall from me, raped me out of serious admiration,
in his parents' bed, he must have really liked me,
I think he talked too much in his life,
had to do with all those women, think the "Doberman" is GAY!

178

When people talk about a God who accompanied them in their shame, looking the tormentor in the eye, as if heaven and hell were both present on earth, the perpetrator punishing himself as a living person, exposed to God's 1000 punishments, but not his mercy, and to his heavenly capriciousness, I saw you running, giving you the burden of never returning, of having no family at all, the bearer of my messages being all the caterpillars from the bushes that I dissected before you. I know smoking can kill. Death leaves nothing behind. Your innocence is my only possession. My legacy to this world.

Strong women scare weak men !
Strong women may act like a Shaolin,
they might appear, but dissappear unseen,
if you don't care or respect, you might find yourself
against the next houses wall !

Cerebellum shrank, Moustache grew, Greeting impossible
Legs free, no matter in bed. On foot, not at feet.
To greet still...the chance straight out!
What do you say to a woman, the mother whose child you stole?
"Personally... I'm going to go and jerk off at home now,
I don't have anything to do with you now,
but you still look quite acceptable?"

Sex addicts show women
every conceivable interest,
in their complexes, their age,
their excess weight, their being tied up,
their frigid nature in bed, their cleaning job,
their messed up past,
their search for the usual routine,
their comfort and uncertainty,
until the day when he himself finally "cracked" them,
then all the others come again.

Married life often depends on one thing,
like the "desire to have children", many mothers say
a real long-term commitment required this,
which can be so massive, the only bonding glue,
the desire to have a family with children,
admittedly greater than the love for the man.

At first it was that, as a child I only played in the forest,
out with animals, ran around naked in neighboring houses,
sat in the bathtub with boys,
that parental violence, and rape of my person,
stopped me 88% of the time from looking for a partner,
and yet it was only when I was thirty
that my biological clock ticked in such a way
that I harbored a desire to have children,
which I managed to realize without a problem.

Women who talk about the joy of motherhood being a reason for
preparation, the child's soul, the body in transformation, the preparation for
birth, the gymnastics, massage and yoga, the wellness therapy, every
preliminary examination, the anticipation of the primal scream, the most
beautiful experience in a woman's life, it hurts the same for every woman,
nothing more, all that nonsense and hocus-pocus didn't interest me, and it
was also agreed that the father would be kept out of it as much as possible
with me and the child.

A woman who has a guy who looks as old as his own mother and is only
looking for a mother in me, if you look at it narrowly, would only be
looking for the woman's comfort, offering her a benefit by being the fighter
herself, she can then arrange everything perfectly, make it look like a
partnership to the outside world for her guy who would rather go out for a
stale beer than commit to his own words, who can't even get it up in bed
anymore, and yet, by ignoring biological facts, a child can come out of it,
and she would have two children on her hands.

I had no family. That is, I thought, it was an advantage to be far away, and not to run the risk of the family claiming my child, even though a simple denunciation was enough, and the distant family deigned to separate me from my child by committing high treason. How could the lawyer honestly have warned me about something like this years ago, when he surely suspected it, because he called my father evil? I don't need a handsome young man. He would have just ordered me, an older woman, to do his housework for him. I never wanted an engineer who would accompany me around the lake on Sundays with a handbag and nice shoes and gloves. I wouldn't have played the role of a breeding machine for a rich guy either, because in the process, dreams and goals, previously studied interests and talents, and wishes for one's own life are completely lost.

The classic woman can count herself lucky that after 15-20 years of being single, someone took pity on her, so as a jack of all trades, she should iron shirts, and when she is lonely in life, in a conservative marriage with a decent job, she should have a conversation or two with people who are poor and living on the streets. So that when she gets home she knows what she owes to her marriage. The man's special wishes such as job, children, household and all everyday tasks, he also wants to have hot meals up to three times a day, and to be served, his only involvement in the evening he sits alone in front of the television.

A society only functions on the backs of women, whose biological clock is ticking, which will always lead women to have to bear and care for children, in this respect, women know by nature that children must be cared for, and they cannot just leave everything as it is, this is what the man who controls relies on, society exists, because women take everything for granted.

A beautiful woman should also have the right to recognize her qualities within herself, to receive only the very best attention that she deserves and to be fulfilled to the moon and back again. If her own husband does not recognize this, she can always look for someone else. A man would do the same.

People's happiness is a tough business, it doesn't just fall from the sky, it's more like it's fished out of brackish water with both hands. Happiness is more like a fairly brief moment, the fiery moon hidden behind clouds, the sun caressing the raven in the light. Happiness is, to put it honestly, what the moment feels, not the garden gnome in the neighbor's ass, even if he hides it behind a hedge as high as a house. I tried. I wasn't suited to judo. As a child, I didn't want to climb on puny little boys I didn't see that as a sport. If there had been judo for one-man operations, then so be it. That way I never ended up in the police club, never ended up as a dead officer, never wasted my years as my father's pride and joy, and was not in my mother's toxic relationship, without forgiveness and forgetting, without retribution and obsession. I was simply worth more to myself !

This morning at the market I said to a woman that she should be modest and ask why she was so wise to only buy the red-cheeked young apples for her grandchildren. This gave me the impression that the lady wanted to teach the children to distinguish between colors. It bordered on racism to teach them to point at all the other colors that they didn't like, instead of simply explaining to them that apples are healthy and nothing else.

At another stand the baker's wife spoke a little more strictly to her only young employee. But I liked both of them. She said to the girl, "You don't have to take it so seriously!" I added, "Nobody has the right to notice something like that, especially when it comes to boys and girls, because it's their main character who always takes everything so seriously because everyone expects it of them! That's exactly what makes them more afraid of "our older generation at this age." The woman grinned respectfully and walked away. The girl thought I was great. I said to her, "She definitely doesn't mean you any harm." "She's actually a really sweet girl!"
What I like about Market is that anyone can and is allowed to just open their mouth. And the other old woman standing behind me could shit her pants because she wanted to order me to take my dog for a short time. I was more of the opinion that it would be better for my dog not to sniff such smelly boots, but I refrained from making the comment.

Otherwise there are also dog owners who stand around in the illusion that they are putting their big, pushy male dog in the way, because They think you just have to walk past them, nodding and greeting them attentively, and they are bursting with anger that I am not even paying attention to them. Oh Susanna, you didn't understand why they were using you? We could watch a film together, in which we grew up together, we almost slept together, there was no male, no female, but childish, where people didn't take the world seriously, only you had everything materially, I had nothing, they never understood, you never wrote back to me, when I asked you why you had condemned me when you were eighteen, so the film followed, unbeknownst to you, that I had to go through hell, because Susanna thought it was appropriate! Eva Susanne experienced deflowering in three different materials, first Brother One, then Brother Two, her great love ended up in the sewage treatment plant, chasing money was her inheritance, but Brother Three just didn't care about her.

German finance minister and his...
good social safety net?
The man seems to be failing at this.
German chancellor largely invisible.
The coalition parties are shitting on each other day and night.
Right-wing extremists are sitting in the Bundestag.
The conservatives are parroting the blue slogans of the Smurf Nazis.
Big tabloid newspapers are inciting hatred against the weakest.
Skilled workers are leaving in droves.
Teachers, nurses and educators are missing,
single parents have to beg for their food,
the trains and buses only run when they feel like it,
the motorways are falling apart,
the army was unable to ward off swarms of mosquitoes,
the televisions only serve quizzes, flea markets and top models,

WHO WOULD HAVE THOUGHT that the Germans are not unhappy?

Unfortunately, I had to relive the farce of my family and the people of my childhood. The racist violence at the moment is very frightening, as is the rise of the extreme right in general, and is reminiscent of the past. Who said: "The only thing we ever learn from history is that we never learn anything from history?" I would no longer even accept the position of visiting professor at a university, for example to provide social science students with something educational about my very full life, teaching that looking away, scientific ignorance, empathic impoverishment should be a signal for high alert, especially in this world! So if I were to present my whole life to the world with its bare truth, and people who don't read found out about it, then people who don't read would simply kill me for my openness, and that would serve no one. But no matter, in the end it all comes down to going your own way and getting a lot out of it, experiencing yourself in it, instead of offering to walk the path at the side of the most beautiful person in you, to serve him, with all admiration.

This is not meant personally against You it is a common saying.
We are the two mighty ones of the earth. You who have everything and I have nothing. Demanding justice is a double-edged sword, what everyone considers to be fair is interpreted differently by everyone. Demonstrating against prosperity is like worshipping the Darkside of the Moon, you walk around its monument and suddenly look at things from both sides, but opening your mouth wide is more about trampling on the freedom that it nurtures and cultivates. I know that people who are in work, are not the worst of our system.

What is more difficult? I regret having spoken. Or regret being silent?

It is more difficult to realize that you are an adult,
but it is easier to become a child again,
because then the burden falls away from you,
and a mother is ready with her fist
to give what is due to anyone who has something against you!

Sometimes you have to make a bad decision to prevent the worst from happening!?

Sometimes love, in its obsession, is not the solution to the solution.
It seems as if we have all dreamed of one thing and then experienced another.

That if I had had singing lessons, if I had performed a series of songs,
if, according to my career, I would have had to fill epics with them but also shatter illusions and hopes ! Then the silence of the night comes to prove to you that the noise is in you, not around you..!!

Finally the legends dissolve within me, finally I walk in dreams,
finally I no longer follow a route, people swim around like this,
places are not recognized precisely, people have no messages for me,
I only know one thing, a rainbow is waiting for me! My luck and I have a lot of understanding, I know it's bad and he knows that I don't have to depend on it.

"Peace is not unity in similarity, but unity in diversity, in comparison and in the reconciliation of differences." -Mikhail Gorbachev-

«You can't have notable victories; but you can be surprised by the twists and turns that will bring you closer». -Antón Chéjov-

"The best way to protect your own secrets is to respect the secrets of others." -José Saramago-

Let us assume that this smallest northern German state has failed miserably with its "experiment".... it was designed with the intention of deliberatcly and deliberately "removing" intelligent people in mind, in order to create a bleak picture that an easy way had been invented for the rest of the sick clientele and the rest of society to scientifically stigmatize, dismiss, observe or justify that it was a German "invention" to talk about inclusion.

185

But to hand these poor people over to the church, to keep them out of all employment and the middle of society and to rent them into houses to intimidate the normal population, in order to observe how much pain people in residential buildings would be prepared to endure, the escapades of the mentally unstable, psychopathic and seizure-prone new residents of a house, without being able to prosecute them in each case, since a district court in all these cases "cases" are not prepared to look behind the "curtain", it is in a way only up to the landlords, who decide who moves into their homes or not. This includes the Diakonie, which keeps a close eye on such separate tenancies, which knows about it, since even a landlord only rarely has the slightest chance or means of bringing these difficult cases to the nuthouse, where they are actually better off, as we know.

But the whole residential chaos distracts from the fact that the intelligent clientele in the northern part of the country, including an expropriation law from the Weimar era, are deliberately having their small children expropriated and, for reasons of power, are being abused in front of their mothers, forcibly weaned over a long period of time, their right to raise them is stolen, even that the outraged mothers are being threatened with prison sentences by the district court if they do not give in and finally give up their children. These mothers are also being portrayed as criminals!

As has already been said in the south of the country by employees of the Diakonie, who have long since retired and describe their work with disabled people, they give the clear impression that in the south there is a widespread view that disabled people of all kinds are more than just pets, incapable of normal cognitive thinking, who are only managed as a side issue.
That mothers in the north get the impression, if only because of the Weimar law, which exists and is applied in the north and which no lawyer ever disputes, that the existence of a child here is accompanied by the same comparative consideration, that children born here are not worth more than a pet, which according to the law is only treated as an object and therefore does not require any special protection! All I can say is that the fat neighbor will remain a narcissistic voyeur to me for the rest of his life, who, when

crossing a red road sign, will stick to his diarrhea and, in my opinion, due to the hidden dictatorship, seen in detail, will never trigger an erotic thought in my eyes, he is simply far too fat for that !

Characters who cope and combat, overcoming their own weaknesses as well as catastrophes spawned by tumultuous times.

I acted pragmatically based on my professional experience
and in a way that was able to keep the balance, but I was fleeced and sent home. They realized that I had skills, but that was not needed there!
Meanwhile, a second applicant... her idea of skills was as follows:

tear-jerker
unfortunate case
pitiful
without skills
not very good at teaching
or technically incapable
but when it comes to colleagues
ready to cause trouble
pointing at others
willing to bully colleagues away
willing to learn to defend herself
She got the brilliant job and contract even today I point out to her as I walk past that working means actually taking action, not pampering the clientele like a speechless stuffed animal after 20 years she could start doing that !
Thanks to not being given a professional opportunity.

I understood from the very beginning that from now on I would not allow a single person to bully me in every situation in my life !

Which this opportunistic woman has failed to do to this day !

The Torn Man,....
on the one hand tender,
on the other hand violent,
on the one hand the cult of friendship,
on the other hand a slight traitor,
the unbelievably attractive beauty,
at the same time so beautiful
that it seemed dangerous,
a relationship with him is not possible,
he only seeks the power struggle, like a narcissist
testing the weakness of his counterpart,
humiliating him, but at the same time reassuring himself,
going for his own profit,
in truth lacking in communication,
but a beast for the cinema, does not feel prevented from
surviving his career in a fascist system
"pettily" to his advantage, that he lives best for himself.

WE KEEP ON ... JUMPING WE COPE
and stay RIDING WE HOLD US DECADES DREAMING !

This is the German woman, always alone, in her lonely little castle,
she could drink dirty water there all her life, and she was always from here,
that's why you always come crawling to her, German stuffed animal,
as your PREY, in sex tourism... just to be able to sniff her out ONE TIME,
and embarrass yourself ! For those who want to know more about the
project – Creation and Solidarity – that I sometimes talk about here in this
old family home. I have noticed that those many ugly owls and brunette
girlies old or young, most time are asit aside the roads and hold eye if that
one and only prince would pick them up, even that they stood aside their
bushes, that one sad and lonely, hurt and angry prince sended out from his
wife, he becomes the prey, even themselves have a husband with kids at
home, those brunette witches love it to hurt and divide partnerships even
their own with a finger snipp.

People being hurt, hurt other's themselves as revenge?
It's no real wonder why those brunette witches did not want my friendship
any of those last 35 years here around, they are to big liars, and fucking
aroung all time. Those guys but do greet me friendly, and their hate grows
pu to that day, they get sooo damn jealousy that i do not fuck around for a
bitch tale, and keep on going, cope and be filling my own carrier, i am just
not inviting the bitches, and not their guys, the rage grows up to the ceiling
and then they throw the guys out of the house. Even these hurt guys
afterwards do no more trust in the women, and would never ever try to
contact me for real, as revenge, as consequence that they keep on fucking
the brunettes.

I AM TOO GOOD FOR THEM ! I AM DENYING THOSE PIMPS, and
DON'T REACT on SILLY BITCH TALK. THAT makes them grow a hate
on all girls who are blond.

I see them meanhwile since so many decades age with me, but those
brunettes from the long therme partnerships with the poor guys under their
authority, the women do only grow fat, and age looking like their own
fathers, they turn to be so damn male looking. The hate culture feeds and
breeds. Indeed they dream in a parntership that all the others would turn to
be a bot of their fantasy. That is called the very old game of conditioned
people. I don't talk a single word to those bitches anymore. I see why this is
kinda maniac, and the bluff and maniac game ends with every broke love
experience, and afterwards you shall see them beg for my sympathy in order
to get a grip on me.... always the same game. If i am a magnet I do not feed
them at all. I know that.
This is like being a good shepard dog, who loves the world, and loves the
girls, and he has good hearted soft mind, a bit tipsy funny balanced and
peaceful, but you shall see those rivals around who just wait and see, when
they meet such a fellow like me, the haters of other dogs, they want to bite
my face and get me out of their ways. I can good feel how a male dog feels,
who is bullied for his good heart.

These are all humans, and they are ambivalent. I may better cope and keep on riding my own horse, and look around from the back of my horse, and don't care of the others. They want to parasite on my strength and sympathy. This told me a lady while shopping today. We spoke about all those sports we did in life. And she was rich and her daughter was an elegant horse riding lady with success. I told her my interest in horses was the very same, too, i learned all about this, but had not money for a horse riding highness and carrier. But that lady said when continuing her way, that we shall keep on riding our horse and.... then she went on. It's not the money that divides the people, it is the same understanding of the good things and worths. Yes, that sounds very true, what she meant with ..... was coming home, and had a big hunger on an oat and linseet, nuts and raisin muesli, that is that feeling that a real mom was speaking then i need my baby brei, and today i met under a tree on a bench three newcoming lawyers speaking with me all to each other in all four directions twenty minutes long, while Mable rested in the shadow, uhhhh hahahaha that was big fun ! That was really funny.

We spoke about the theory of ambivalent people, that causes that students of law are needed, and if all were people with such a scientific brain, they would make this a good world, or otherwise the humans were all the same, then possibly half of them were corrupt.

We spoke about the violence and murderers who cause the need in police, who had no job without it.

We spoke about the studied medical area who just most time are needed for all those poor ones being cut and beaten to pieces in violence and broken teeth, so that the docs must repair all these.

We spoke about those jurists who are seemingly like tourists all over the place but never at one place the second time, and i said, that it is a pitty how far old people have to walk to their bank account missing their eyes to use the online banking, and be so old and broke on the long ways they have to go, but here in the north the climate is so appropriate and privilegues, that you see the most broken elderly with sticks and help who still smiles all over the face enjoying the summer day. And i told about this one stupidiest lady i met for this year, who shaved the perfect fur of a labrador mix twice a year, sothat he would join the hot weather better, but the result is, after shaving that hair grows even triple more, and he looks like a black ice bear with fur ten centimeter thick, and almost dies in the sun.

You may think all this bouncing around in a fast paced talk, back and forth, like a verbal dance! Was it like that? No, this was only all my saying, as you know me. These young guys had to listen to me, then Mom has left them thinking about it, yes, started with my saying that a woman i was friend to, once she said, that i definitely had to study medicine, then i bought such english books about the wisdom for physiotherapy and english big study, we don't have that in german, we only have our small massage therapist with a few therapies learned in two years a small practical course with anatomy, and the look out for other places to learn more, but the result was that i tried to learn that teaching in english, with german understanding and Latin words, and it was nothing for my brain, not possible !!! FUCK in don't have that mind and brain to study, first of all would be that i had to rape my mind before start, as you say it, that bunch of foreign words, and explanations, three languages to follow in one thought, and then all medicine knowledge that exists, i say - WOW - it is possible for other people, you just keep on learning and never find out of the books again, imagine with such a mind and brain you walk throught the streets afterwards ????

It is just the ONE THING, to do it or not to do it, the brain is not ready for YOU, you use it, then training and discipline without give up the flow. But what you say, is altime that you are a little afraid to use your own thought, opinion, speech, wording, to express yourself. People find "the bombardment from all directions make me doubt shaping opinions I can say is all mine". I know this is not a mistake, you never learned to take the hammer and blow it on the pizza and smash the whole table, without that knowledge to ruin the others opinion while being stronger than the storm, helps no way, you have to become a fighter in order not to drown.

191

You shouldn't hate a person if they don't look at the world through your eyes. Heaven loves the heart and sincerity, but not sober calculation. The world is changing at a tremendous speed, all living beings are beginning to feel this, only narrow-minded people or those who deceive themselves and others continue to follow the same path. Everyone is concerned about their own problems, a rare person thinks about the affairs of his neighbor. Love is a gift of one's innermost soul to another so both can be whole.

My Bros
My Heart
My Twins
My Siss
My Sons
My Sun
My Life
My TWINS - Nakedness is the gift of the skin, the empty page given to writing ; it is to be touched for the voracious and always renewed first time of mouth and fingers. Strong women aren't born, they are made by the storms they walk through.

What kind of crap is that? A jasmine scented candle...
Shut up, you scoundrel, your father-in-law looks like a burglar.
I still have something to do, I'll be right back. Happy name day, your chair was from the sex mascot. Today the weather in Brazil's city is full of sunshine. The name Raoul is the most celebrated, let's drink !
The fact of the honeymoon with the fake man, the moustache and children. By the way, will we see each other tomorrow after the fake bachelor party? A group of drunken women broke into a mosque in Marrakesh, stole the shoes of the people praying, and accidentally killed a man. Being stuck on a toilet bowl as a fraud is ultimately not nice either. Would end the first night of marriage by saying yes, with full confidence that the air around them would stand still when they looked at each other from then on, and there would never be another chance to lie to each other in a drunken gleeful way.

To artificially let the wind blow around their ears as if it were a staged event, and to manipulatively swear to eternal honesty. For wonderful reasons, this is the rare opportunity for strangers to make the groom their prey, to catch him like a fish, and to joke about stealing him from the right bride, simply because he has a beautiful beard like Don Juan. The two at the altar were not immune to the hard blow of fate, when it was observed that their long, slim legs would one day become round and fat, their breasts would sag, and the peace and harmony in the house would be disturbed, until betrayed love and loyalty finally burst like a pot. It was a good thing that the children fell from the sky anyway, because they had simply become too heavy for the busy stork in the air. But the little ones end up lying just like their parents.

Some lie while dancing around the fire. Others open the first party to celebrate the most sought-after single of all time, who everyone is fighting over. He takes up virtually every seat at the table of committed relationships and shatters the domestic peace until fists fly. After all, there is no guarantee of great love until you can see in the video that a fake wedding with the parents presented was just a fake. The new porn queen can cry.
And the party is over, after everything that cost. If you look past it, you are actually not incapable of understanding all of this, otherwise men lie to cheat on their wives, but they also lie to each other as divorcees and pretend to remain friends. Putting on a show for each other for decades is a show of love, nothing more, no comment on that, even if they would like to jump into my face like parasites from the sidelines, even though they will never know me! The deceitful children who put on a play don't start dating like those who only get married many years later when they are more mature. That doesn't make a difference!

No, i am not political, just against all very cruel, corrupt and dangerous people, misogyn and antidemocrates, i had just made my life experiences, that made me so truly speaking, but never mind.

Kindful to ask be about work... but they fired me long ago, and i had done all so good. Sothen i started to write down my life, working experience, poetry, and philosophy, my view of emancipation, my finding thought about marriage, and dates, my loyality to my son still, my labrador dog, even i took revenge to my family experierence that i left 40 years ago, and some novels, some things about healing, my working areas were in the physiotherapy in the elderly care, the work with handicapped people, kitchen work, house cleaning, horses, and.... i know if people do such different things a life through it sounds a bit much, has no big worth in germany, so at the end they call you all "competent indeed" but give you no work, the most years in my life i worked for free, but i am aware of my worth and know my pledoyer. The publishing of all in all with good 120 books came in the row ten years ago. I know it sounds impossible, my brain works like a machine, my dreams have worked out with me so much.

I like Nature Boys, my uncle was one long ago, he came from here, with irish, Cherokee parents born in germany, went with the Aunt to Maryland, then Utah, then California, he was first soldier, then cared for the woods, and studied engineering, then made a company to clean the drinking water, ... he is jumping around in Asia and Australia now, with his new girl friends, and his wife, my Aunt asit alone in California at home, being upset, that place she lives is called "Rescue" that sounds so funny, she gets in rage, when seeing her walls alone, and finds almost that house as cage, and knows nobody privately. I mean this is a tragedy, to early marry, and then have the search for freedom.

The roots you have give you a perspective, it is like a warm feel of the ancestors. You know i have not written just like that, i have such a huge fantasy, that i dreamed of times far back to the stonegde and those nice people lived in caves in Africa, so then once I saw in dream an old couple just ride along my house here on the saddle back of a huge black dinosaurier. My roots are also native indian so that i walked in dreams in woods with the wilderness, and climbed the mountains and then took off flying, i may feel to be the grass in the valley and i may see humans flying.

194

I may find rescue in nature in many ways to enter the nature in dreams. I love Nature, no do not believe now i am not a real american native indian, it is my imagination only, these places may also happen in North Scandinavia. Have some friends there, a little part of family too, i have to go my own way, i am not begging for their hospitality. Good ok, now you see, that i am not rich, and the lesser a family owns, she cannot bring out all those world wide travels around the globe just to vistit all parts of family.

MY FAMILY is ONE MOM, that is ME, and ONE SON that is 27 JULIAN, and ONE 80 year old tight friend in the next town, who was my sonny boys chosen friend and father by willing. I like travelling, it is good, germans say "Ohne Moos nix los" like now i haven't the penny to make vacancy. Then look at the european chaos, in all those many countries travel those asylants in suffer and danger, and those nazis, who have all against them, then too those climate changes cause in many vacancy places big fires, and the landscapes change, they build more frontiers, and i think that travelling as such, like i knew it 1982 in comparison today, is much more dangerous.

Those times when i was seventeen, i tramped, and was welcome really EVERYWHERE, as volontairy worker, and just to be guest, asking for a place to stay, i could go EVERYWHERE in the south and almost to GAZA, and the way back i slept with a Kanadian Woman in one Sleeping bag, she looked like me and we hitchhiked from Israel back to almost the adress at home together, but without sex. Working in those times was for stay and get food nothing more, that keeps for ever the feeling of WHAT SUNSHINE MEANT. Meanwhile i see always in every house under roof someone had died.

Why search the seas?
Why swim in streams?
Why look for a shady forest pond?
Why disappear into quarry ponds?
Why go mudflat hiking at low tide?

For whose sake... through the glasses...
but do you like the chlorine chicken swimming pool
with chips on your feet,
with cigarette butts in the grass,
with smelling bath oil on fat bellies,
with sandy blankets,
with long-legged Barbie doubles,
with wasps on your Fanta,
with sideburns and swimming trunks,
with the moped peeping tom,
with secretly photographing tits,
with making a big splash
in a thong on the edge of the pool? Ask yourself that!

What is real? Jewelry bought is of no value.
Jewelry exchanged remains of real value.
What is fake? Travel to the country where the sun always shines.
Having to return to the country where the cold unites them.
A little bit of fake is everywhere,
from the violin to the sound of the angels,
the stage is too far away, the songs sink into the river.
Where is the tour going? On the highway, into the gutter and back.
On the long drinking tour, and impregnating an angel.
Who doesn't count as a father?
He who only knows the drug himself.
How should he know the suffering of the children,
whose lives he has beaten to the core.

I don't function as kitt anymore for broken relationships, and as positivity
while surgeons, and help to find out of alcoholism, as answer how sex
funcitions, as explaining how to understand reality, what all about their
sickness, deseases, and mental problems, an intelligent woman gets abused
all kind in the networx. The most sooo loyal friendly people do suck me out.

In the first years i fell with that trap often, and really tried to believe in a lifelong friendship, so made many packages of friendship presents to such people. We may talk here but never again talks to strangers on my phone. Thanxxx so are you mature being enough to understand that. I myself have been through a series of Wrong friendships. Who did not ? Nowadays i so do only watch the people outside and see through all the fake and theater they play with others hearts. I mean there are most time kids in the game, and i find that so superficial. Life can be unfair, ohhh dear, i see this hurt too, when see the wives and women try to break people's hearts, they only do it in order to stay in the main role of the flesh game, i don't like women, who play around their pussy, and then go home to the husbands and play the mom and daddie's best horse in the stable. When i notice such an example i do not communicate to such anymore. And i see those Moms also raise a bunch of kids and do not even care, if one daughter runs out in the street with just 13 years old and tried to find friends to talk to, enters in strange doors inside to guys and gets raped ? Then finds herself in therapy, but no more scool, then pregnant, therapy off, child gone, and at least a junkie, they are Moms who like to fuck, and all kids come out with the same names all started with "J", the kids some of them get brought to another family to have a real life, then meet me on the road, and speak about that real Mom like she was the worst they ever had. So small kids with the mind to speak about their Mom „the slut", she did destroy all the most just because of her behaviour. Ach, i know how fast a child has to understand the real side of the life, too. My Mom was just cold as ice, that was no problem, but aside of two golden sisters i was the one who was bullied and beaten. No, as people know and say, that a strong woman first needed to become strong while she was walking through the storm. If that sounds wise, yes, but much of the truth tells, if women so privileged find all Love they recieve, and good comfort, and safety and trust as long as they show that they never had a reason to be greatful, to share such a luck instead of recieve hate, like othcrs do, so these conveniant ones are most time those who let the others fall in love. I know it if you once fell so hard, then you are busy dreaming a character you met, and get rid of those, nobody wants altime dreaming of the people with the bad sides explained in the dreams so often, why that ?

People think people are scared of the Truth. So scared, They'll choose lie over truth. Over and Over again, yess, as many as people live on earth, they are damn right. I see this more often that a youngster who complains a while in his first little puberty life crisis, and starts overthinking that one person needed just a second of a flash in his heart and brain, and the first monumental thought brings out his fantastic view of a future without pain, in knowing what he likes and loves the most ! Those kids with the damn fears first, loose that thing and see, that fear as such is a fake, those become value people when getting old.

Love and peace are the paths that lead to Paradise, but only love is the key that opens its gates. (Paradise Lost)

Only when we love can we know eternity, because in love, time disappears. To love is to live with the heart. Hold my hand...take me where time has no place. Hold it tight when life is difficult.

- Hermann Hesse -

My Dear One in Oklahoma. I slept a night over that marriage proposal. I said in the beginning caused by my life, i am hesitating to agree in such an event. I keep on listening inside my heart, that i have doubt. That nothing to do, that you own a brilliant style telling me this, and belong into a fantastic future life with all your earning, and nature's comfort around you, if i am not willing, as well knowing by myself, i am not prepared in a marriage in this one whole life. These were others who destroyed it, not you. It made me fall into a deep abyss, that i am not willing to enter. I am so sorry for you have had such a nice wording at me, and i hope you will be in your country far more lucky telling the right one the truth how your heart is beating. Just that sight of a mans warm embrace cannot be enough for me to leave the whole continent, and land in a total other system of thinking and believing, and i was hurt to much in life, to survive without this rooted feeling, that i fought for so long time. My roots are my survival, the rest of me is knowing that i will spend in loneliness but in a way to love, the love and peace to feel.

But the start of a partnership needs the love to be affected, and in a distance of 10.000 miles i were never convinced that a total step like that was the right for me !

Love and Peace. Eternal Selflove. Patience until night. Forget about it all.
The waterfall for All. The Motherland for you and me.
Welcome to the roots. Entering and write on the skin.
That Love is all around. These scars wouldn't be so hidden
if you would just look me in the eyes.

Let us be grateful to people who make us happy, they are the charming gardeners who make our souls blossom. - Marcel Proust.

They say here that humor is conditional,
assuming that both have the same knowledge,
it was a real pleasure for them, I reply "likewise",
even without living in the castle, not practicing the "high art horsemanship"
to this day, despite everything, happy "if they were still with us tomorrow!"

You are welcome to their meal.
They put on deer antlers.
They let the housewife have her way.
They are waiting for you in the middle of the plate.
As if today's house speciality was
the "False Snake" served in buffalo skin.
I passed my recipe on to the world a long time ago,
but I don't know if the world wants us to save it?
When they're done with you,
do they feel like you were welcome,
uniquely "Jolie très loin." but also "Très loin la Jolie!"

- Heike Thieme - Ylva -

I look around, "Holland" is so popular !
Anyone who has been there, even someone who was born there,
wants to go back home to the Netherlands,
just without any obligation,
"Welcome here, you Dutch people !" now we have a problem,
if the influx to Holland, a stream of refugees
from Holland to us due to the climate, would soon be barely noticed,
as the seas are rising, and that will happen tomorrow,
it will hardly be noticed in Germany,
where we all know that German bureaucracy
is one of the SLOWEST in the world !

GDR plus BRD together in a two months Marriage
decided after a LasVegasParty with 15 Martini, as thanks
as quick as loss of Emanzipation,
as sure as passed equality in job,
as far as bye to Kindergarden free,
as sure as less than half in politic,
as small the balance in business,
as other directed military,
in the socalled West inherit millions in the socalled East inherit frustration !
In the West, the paternal iron hand rules,
whoever does not have a career will lose out,
8 million unemployed, the iron hand remains immobile,
in 2024 such conditions will spread,
work bans will spread, people long for work,
the unemployed want social security, but women do not work,
single parents certainly not, unless they are converted and opportune,
all those condemned to poverty will be stigmatized and bullied.

I don't want to know what you ate last week.
We're sitting in the car, you're driving to Florence for your engagement.
I want to go to Florence too, so there's nothing to say.
I want to visit my boyfriend in Venice.

I'll sit there in silence for three days,
until he just shows up. This leaning tower there,
is as certain as the fact that I'm hungry, and I'll just take some,
from the conveyor belt in the student cafeteria,
from the plate whose remains a man left behind.
On the island, words are not in demand,
better than being chased by tourists in Venice.
Has anyone ever experienced
that a child born here in the country is welcomed,
is considered protected from the law,
is protected from arbitrary treatment, kidnapping, abuse? NOISE!!
As true as the current Instagram voice message is,
is welcomed more than ever, nothing is noticed anymore,
this message ends with the death of the person
who sent this message to me 70 years ago !

How someone ticks ! The way we meet, in such an inexplicable way,
you often get the impression of who you are dealing with just
by looking at them. You don't need a foto lens to see how someone ticks.
Most of the time it's just about making yourself known,
broadening your horizons, as slaves to our own neurons
and determinants that lead to chaos.
Could we even claim to be anything other than ourselves?
The rounds I will still make, whose requests I will not refuse,
will be those that know how to keep quiet !

.... what I am currently writing, it is almost ready, it is funny to bring out
myself a round thought dedicated just to me, as if someone had warned me
not to bring out to the common publicum the total truth of a person herself,
will end with killing that person by people who usually are no readers and i
will give it a hard cover, and some good pictures is now my private Heike
book, just as I had written a beautiful children's book that contained the key
words for my son and for me. This book now contains my key words for
me. It is almost finished.

201

It is fun to come up with a complete thought that is dedicated only to me.
I think that the water that I used all my life,
which was used to clean other people's toilets,
you could have tried yoga or messed around with wellness, I say
then you wouldn't have had to do your breasts,
I think in the end it's more a matter of stopping the concept and engineers
who ensure the preservation of drinking water, getting the patent,
as I have always considered good, to be a little more caring!

Since I say that I don't like her, and therefore just keep my distance,
nobody could ask me to approach you, if you have just hurt me!
Do I let myself be shown up, and used?
Or do I break away from this toxic relationship, and end it?
That is why I am separating from Germany.
That is why I am not looking around for you.
Because I see for myself what I am going to change in my life.

So, why are SOME white people ashamed of their immigrant ancestry?
They fear the confrontation to fears.
They ask for understanding their fantasy.
They beg for proposals uncritical.
They want the convenient easiest way.
They hope for a Total Acceptance all days.
They like to use others gifts but no greatfulness.
They adore to play power to unkown people.
They watch Europeans a little pittiful.
They may use us and love, but let us fall.
They show up their extensions and comfort.
They end with a big meal, and we belong to the farts.
But no one is interested in our history.
They pretend to be themselves the sun dawn.

THAT's WHY NOT !!!

The little girl statue outside the local church had a cover on by unknown street artist today. But it is true to bring a blanket on over a child statue in order to let them all far good see, that there are worser things to be seen under the surface and the naked statue of a child that all pass ignorantly is an affront.

COLLECTIVE SUICIDE? Fun Facts - the country in 5th place worldwide:
over 9 million Germans have problematic alcohol consumption,
over 1.6 million are addicted, over 74,000 alcohol deaths per year,
economic costs due to alcohol consumption amount to €57 billion annually,
every drunk can personally choose where their organ failure begins,
whether it is a fatty liver, coronary arteries, brain vessels, all arterioles,
thrombocytes in the lymphatic vessels, intestinal activity,
everything is destroyed in its function, the body starves and becomes fat
at the same time, it craves nutrients, which are no longer absorbed,
but all the toxins accumulate in it like a time bomb,
the skin changes, the muscles, bones, simply everything,
YES and by the way, people become Neanderthals,
if they also drink away their qualities in the frontal cortex,
and are no longer capable of natural inhibition !
I forgot to say, that alcohol is also a Neurotoxin, destroys the nerves.

RIDICULOUSNESS!
Now someone tell me that the choice of words was wrong,
when the 1.7 heavily addicted people said to the rest of society,
"They're all just jealous!" The sick people, who have been accustomed to neurotoxins through advertising, family influences, tradition, upbringing with pacifiers in beer, "They're not even the worst!" increased health costs of all those who have to suffer from chronic breakdown, psychological brutalization, social withdrawal, systematic decline,
and half of them die from the pure poison, that doesn't stop politics,
when it costs society €57 billion annually, brings €3 billion in tax revenue?
To advertise the poison in the form of a 1 liter bottle of liquor for just €3.50, and to get young people over 14 to drink it??

THAT'S WHAT PEOPLE CALLED THE FDP!!!

You go to work in the morning. You realize, oh, how your head hurts!
They didn't even notice.
How old you have become since you were drinking.
You didn't even know it when you were drunk. You just needed more and
more, and in the end, three questions always remain unanswered:
"Do you want to know what alcohol can do to people?"
"What is better, puke or shit in the doorway?"
and "Where does the path lead?" probably to ....
Try to imagine how they eat their rolls on a Sunday morning
in the HUNSRÜCK, they first have to ride down into the river valley
on the C'est quois ca?, avoid the moped on the bend,
deal with the cloud in the sky like Montezuma's revenge,
everyone has the thought that waking up on a Sunday
in the HUNSRÜCK is a rude awakening!

I am a free thinker. I am happy with it and will be accommodating in the
next life! Life consists of what you have already experienced and the
busyness of making other plans. There is nothing to learn from success.
Everything is learned from mistakes. Are you laughing about that?

Mother Nature said: Let us forgive and forget the torments, it pulled him or
me there right after birth, Not exercising any human rights, robbing a
newborn of his peace, violates 17 long years of catastrophe, robbing him of
peace from all sides, but disillusionment, life can be easily broken. Step
forward, abuse power and let me watch - that is her motto.

Restriction ! If you consider who is out there running around so freely,
you should be advised how to raise someone like this better,
if you consider how often violence is used against children,
with the result that...the direct path to success was blocked !
It is unfortunate that the "child" at 60 does not even come up with the idea
of „thanking" for it, the "child" should be happy when he grows up,

Spending breakfast in the dungeon,
but spending "time together" should not be in the dungeon,
the word for "prison, dungeon" comes from Low German
and is derived from "losing" at addresses
where empathy was not applied so laboriously,
and high treason crawled out of every hole.
The late-born grandchild is denounced as a fetus and is lost.
There're already almost 24,000 arguments against violence against children !
The unwanted daughter, who was not born as a son,
who was declared to be 30% rejects,
so that the "rest" is enough for democracy,
is now called "idolized" and trampled on,
so that she would be "UNPLEASANT"
for all other men for the rest of her life !

The story says, we are doing something for little people,
we are looking for a new script writer,
we are making better politics with less money,
if we knew that the world was going to end tomorrow,
I would still cut down a tree today, we are saving those who want it
in our imagination like in the movies, like Netflix in terms of feeling,
that's what it all means, "Take good care of yourselves!"

I see them as related too,
they have their backs to the wall,
they follow the vines to liven up,
they don't recognize any family,
they bear the burden of money,
they are blinded by Hawaiian shirts,
they only inherit things to block out,
they fall like bottles,
they rest on doing nothing, but their out-and-out psychopath
makes a summer compote out of it all, he painted them a script,
people will still be talking about it in 100 years !

Instead of "Plant a tree !"

The story tells us, „We are doing something for little people", that is what people with an agenda say, socially political or on the extreme right,

„We are looking for a new script writer", what people from the conservative corner say, we already had the thing with the chosen "big strong man",

„We are doing better politics with less money", that is what people say who understand marriage as nothing more than showing off their diamonds, if we knew that the world was going to end tomorrow,

„I would cut down a tree today", that is what people say who even in fantasies of doom want to make a profit for themselves,

„We save in fantasy like in the film, everyone who wants it",
that is what people say whose children come from the piglet factory, from the elite farms, and not from this world, like Netflix of feeling, all of this wants to say, "Take good care of yourselves !"

When my heart breaks and the thirst to have you explodes in my soul, and my being splits in two and I die a little more, when I feel that you are absent, my love, I will no longer go back to listen to your sweet voice whispering to me „the wind, life". I will not be able to see myself reflected in the look of your eyes, we will have to... separate.

That's why i don't want to become a taxi driver !
Hey, there are always enough reasons for people to have to leave when they can no longer find what they want. For them, there are at most dropout shops to work in. That makes it clear to me, I would say, that you no longer feel anything when you have too much social participation.

Even if companies leave their field because of right-wing politics in the East. All of this shows that it is no longer an issue for women here alone, or single parents who are deliberately suppressed in poverty, they always want to leave.

But keeping these parts of the population propertyless is their only motive, to prevent almost half of them from leaving the country immediately if their wallets could afford it. Anyone who manages to leave their chains behind and take off, I congratulate them with distinction! What keeps you here?

Kind regards, Heike

Hey, there are always enough reasons for people to have to leave when they can no longer find what they want. For them, there are at most dropout shops to work in. That makes it clear to me, I would say, that you no longer feel anything when you have too much social participation. Even if companies leave their field because of right-wing politics in the East. All of this shows that it is no longer an issue for women here alone, or single parents who are deliberately suppressed in poverty, they always want to leave. But deliberately keeping these parts of the population without property is their only motive, to prevent almost half of them from leaving the country immediately if their wallets could afford it. Anyone who manages to leave their chains behind and take off, I congratulate them with distinction ! What is keeping you here? Kind regards, Heike Yes, what is keeping you here? I would say the little miracles. That you don't just give up and look away. I keep encountering little miracles. And then you're off in a different direction.

Knowing that there are little miracles, you go through the day more openly. I think that you don't get what you want or dream of in life, but sometimes and only sometimes what we get is more valuable and beautiful than what we dreamed of. The trick is to recognize this and to be able to accept and allow it.

Take me, for example, I met a mother, my neighbor and the sweet little one. Sophie is a little miracle. And the more time I spend with the little one, the more in love I am. I had a great idea recently, well, me and my ideas. I unpacked my classical guitar and played the little one a few classical pieces to help her fall asleep. Boy, boy, did the little one listen attentively, she really liked that. And they are little miracles. We should see things through the eyes of children more often. Forget all our thinking for a moment and just be amazed.

That's exactly what I feel in Schleswig-Holstein, as you say, but it's been the little miracles since 1990 that haven't stopped me from carrying on living, from not giving up! As you say, finally someone has understood it, and just like you, I encounter young families with all their babies these days, as you describe, because the children react so charmingly, so open to the world, spontaneous, loud, brave, curious to the point of bursting. It's them, all the children, who enchant our world and let everyone take part in it, if you let them, it's nice that you see it the same way !

240 times in northern Germany, a woman was prepared for the fact
that before the birth of her child, plans were being made
to take her child away from her without her knowledge,
bring it back to her, even before child was abused !

PEOPLE, WHAT IS KEEPING YOU HERE?
Is that a reason for a Pope?
To build his Vatican so high,
as if the voyeur were only interested in
seeing all the abuse around him
with his own eyes, watching the little children in his care,
even those who are his own, doing it, through his large WINDOW,
so that the commander of divine sparks finally gets satisfaction,
until he himself is thrown down from the high tower
after he has cast the children himself into hell in a rampage,
he jumps into the depths with them?

Go feed the unicorns and paint the world in bright colors. And if you can't see any unicorns right now, then go and look for the child, then you can see unicorns again. And other wondrous creatures too. That should mean your inner child.

maybe I'll find a real tree ball that enchants me
maybe I'll find the dream stones that I dropped while doing a pee
maybe I'll find that little cloud again that hasn't been there for so long
maybe an eagle will sit by my side again
maybe the toddler of a single mother will grab me
so that I'll philosophize maybe a really old memory
from my early childhood will pop into my mind
maybe the voice of an ancestor will reach me as he waves to me
maybe I'll grab the branch I'm sitting on with a rope attached
and swing myself into the distance ! I wish you all the same, you good
friend and also Leek, who you never use with me.

Best Wishes, Heike

Business people looking for a partner, such a person acts like an advertising expert who sends his ex as an old story to meet him, to appear interesting! But be careful when choosing a partner.
You are presenting them as a potential customer,
they only expect you to jump on their feet
for a few claims that you make,
for all the extensions, if the deal falls through for them,
they drop you as a bad investment or like a hot potato!
The most beautiful praise covers up the fact
that in reality you are worth nothing to them
in the common sense of the word,
you would only suffer damage from them,
and the greatest possible damage at all.
The Swedes, compared to the Germans,
are excellent at this and know it all, be warned !

Love each other. Whether you're too right or too left.
Everyone has a racism problem. Not everyone in uniform is a racist.
Some are just postmen!

Brat Kamala Harris ! You Are a damn studied professionell !
I'm Aware a Woman with Authority ! You Are best in direct speech !
I am counting on You in every Week !
You stand where others hang in the Trees !
I am feeling a fresh nice Wind in Democracy !
You stand for Freedom, the Elderly, stand for Water and Life surrounding !
I am willing to Vote an Accurate Being.
No one will bring me to another inner holding. I am fighting FOR that value
You stand for ! You Are the One bring the Real Life further !
I AM LOVING KAMALA HARRIS, as if YOU ARE A SISTER OF MINE,
and A YOUNG ONE !!! Blessings from Germany, Heike !
The politics that Harris is carrying out are not superficial.
Where she previously fulfilled expectations,
she did so out of a sense of duty. Investing abroad is an argument.
Where civil structures are strengthened, as foresight in politics demands,
influxes are actually reduced. She did what she was instructed to do.
No one can blame her for that !

Landing ! The stork may land there.
But no one can take me back to the dungeon,
an old abandoned castle, from the Middle Ages,
just behind it a ruin, over which I fled,
people talked about the old bars on the windows,
it was supposed to be my current home,
with idiots, whores and murderers,
in which the family threw me after the rape!

Loneliness is not fatal, my friend What kills me is drowning in human
lies..?? If death takes me and we don't meet, don't forget that I really wanted
to meet you.

If the unicorn beckoned to me, then I never sank before it,
if it told me not to be afraid of me,
because the unicorn has grown with the years,
if the unicorn promises me what the heart says to it,
I will remain faithful to it.

How did your relationship with the person you preferred to everyone else
end? _ "I let go a little to prove that I was the one who held on. And it all
ended..." I know a peepee ends, a smile from the moon ends, a day in peace
ends, a music with me ends, a terribly good love ends, a flood of tears ends,
a longing for more endings.

On the sidewalk of life. There are leaves that have turned yellow after once
being beautiful; They began to fall from our souls; There is no water to
bring them back to life and there are no strong branches to hold on to;
This is how we humans are;

No matter how much you care about the person, do not ask them to treat you
the way you want, because each person treats you according to the position
you occupy in their heart.

Do not listen to anyone who frustrates you or belittles your ambitions.
Who showers you with his attention, create a home for him in your heart
that suits only him. The actions of people change their position in our hearts.
The soul tends towards those who share sadness, fatigue and difficult days
with it, but in joy all people are loved ones. It seems like we all dreamed of
something... and then came across something else.

Tell those who think they know you: "Don't think you have gone deep, for
you have not gone beyond the edge of the beach."

Rest assured that marriage is truly beautiful if you marry the right way.

Accusation !

If I had the money and the right partner at my side, I would sue you
for mistreatment, traumatizing, bullying behavior, denial, slander,
failure to provide assistance in an emergency,
constant family persecution, wrongful dismissals,
for invisible bullying at work,
for standing in the way of a professional career,
the hopelessness of financially emancipating myself,
even for breach of contract, deprivation of my freedom,
for hitting your own child in front of everyone else,

but don't take it personally, father!

Without hope, without sadness. He holds his head down.
Wearily he crouches on the wall. Wearily he sits there and thinks:
Miracles will not happen. Everything stays as it was.
If you don't see anything, you won't be seen.
If you don't see anything, you're invisible.

Steps come, steps go. What kind of people are they?
Why doesn't anyone stop? I am blind and you are blind.
Your heart sends no greetings from the soul to the face.
If I didn't hear your feet, I would think you didn't exist.
Come closer! Sit down, until you sense what blindness is.
Lower your head and lower your eyelids,
until you know what was foreign to you.

And now go! You're in a hurry !
Act as if nothing had happened.
But remember this line:
"If you don't see anything, you won't be seen."

- Erich Kästner -

Organized abuse !
SUCH an idea had to be "born" first !
THE CHURCH provides, and trivializes and covers up to this day.
THE OFFICE hands over the children, and other abusers profit.
THE COURT approves ARBITRARY ACTION, and lawyers all wave it off.
THE MOTHERS have to watch, and the NUMBER of these atrocities,
are relativized by blaming the MOTHERS.
THE ABUSERS of SMALL CHILDREN,
act in such a LINE that CHILD ABUSE
is seen in the WAY BEHIND THE CURTAIN, like with MURDER -
there would no longer be any TALK OF AFFECT,
if attention were paid to the CHILD CASES!

What do they say?
The poor children in the country have no right to exist,
no birthright, no protection from violence, no right to their own mother,
no constitution to protect them both, but the guarantee...
snitched on, and slaughtered, knockout drops and off they go,
to be abused at least once in their life, as small as they are,
and are not allowed, can, will,.... defend themselves, or whatever,
we are all screwed....What does the church still say today?
What kind of country is this, says the pedophile, just for "LOVE"
when you can't have any joy?

Go after the women.
Sexism from all sides.
German craft of bullying.
Faking the flat, lame letter
"social worker".

The knockout drops always in the bag.
The slightest parrot, the report is in the bag, and you can at least call
yourself a "social worker". Then you have carte blanche to denounce
everyone from the lowland country !

LEGACY

How do you auction off a prop,
when, out of convenience, the next fuck,
whoever wants it, is on the third floor, room 2755, at 2:00 pm?
how do you still deny Corona today,
when some people have already had it four times?
how do you open your pants in front of the Pope,
when the whole fuck is standing around it?
how do you open a dark door,
when it has never been opened for a long time?
how do you lead a weirdo life,
when you're still at home with mom and dad?
how can one indulge in stupidity,
when it's just for entertainment for others?
how do you spot a pair of eagles, when you're flat out
can't see the forest for the trees?
how does a healthy bird talk to you, when it's really just your uncle?

I have just seen a unicorn yesterday with Mable. A unicorn ! We went
outside to watch how is the unicorn looking out there. When we met the
second truly reliable woman with her beautiful little daughter and dog
outside, the second one i trust. When she started to speak about the theme
paranoid woman and her speech and deeds, i just informed her and the
daughter the exact story to complete our sight of such ones, the hers is more
ending in fashist paranoid speech, and the here one is more psychopath and
hateful as neighbor.I call the first both unicorns to get to know better slowly
the two daughters of two alone educating moms, i like them and they do
react altime tolerantly and trusting in me, their daughters are my first two
unicorns. Then yesterday we sat here inside on the dogs corner in resting
peace, while i almost started to have on real negative thought but just as
they always do to protect me and understand the real side of life, not to
think or use the reason thought again, we got visit of one big young and
beautiful butterfly in the room. I knew they would come this year, the day
before they surrounded me, too, my lovley fellows.

From then on Mable and i started to watch the little wonder, and i spoke to her "You know my babe, what we learned again from this ? That it's always good to stay on the positive path. We both are staying without violent thought, then the fairy, and wonders to see, this little unicorn for example, it looked almost like a little kindful bird. "And Mable loves birds. I told her not to harm a butterfly who is our visit again ! She is my brilliant dog who understands my wordings always, and she knows to treat that visit with care. She is almost 100% violentless my dear one, and today i kept the peace to start a new thought to a novel book again, finally, just started the real writing it down, and functions.

I know such people too, from time to time Rocco, who wants to enter Sweden next year, with the damage done, he told, that might be, if he stands at that point to never wanting come back to germany, and live more in the wilderness, that might happen. That is why Swedes never share much visiting german friends, they find their own nation much better, and more use us as far friends. Only the stupid ones who have such a childish fairys impression aware of the fantasy land of the viking get really bad impressed to get fooled by that lie. We have to get it like that. But we all know such experiences in the rest of the world, too. I wonder if the Germans will learn never to wish for anything from outside their borders, or we're fucked.

I know if people are acting childish, egoistic and self enlighted, that they parallel are strongly hurting others. That way locking the people then let them fall, is almost a typical way of behaviour of the US americans. The copy of America of course we have it since the industrial revolution, but the superficial people will never ever get to know germans as such, not in real, because they would never have reached to cross the border of the sea. Yes, we germans mostly earn just a worldly friendship in a light friendship way. Let us keep it like that. I am not able to be angry about a level and fact that reminds me to kindergarden.

With one thought trapping in the mourn, sorrow and deep feeling of guilt, it is not the consequence to make it all better, if you would punish just the lonely one in you, if you did it, none would profit of it. You single one are not the system, not the society in one person, not the cultural sight of all. Imagine one person like you, and you owned for guarantee at least on the world seven others who are looking and being exactly like you are, but would seldom have that chance to meet them all at one time one place, but for sure that all of them have an own individual thought, and love for anyone else, and go the own ways in life, we CANNOT all be the same good or bad.

That's why better to always think in a positive way, and not torture another ones though by negativity and judgin people to be dead, when there are losses the follow.

Maybe the women here don't want to have children anymore !
Maybe it's time to teach the pig how to lose properly !
THE IMAGE OF A JESUS IN THEIR EYES IS ONLY
BLACK AND WHITE! Your word in God's ear, then get down to business.

I knew the wording in which I was pregnant and reported to the authorities by the strange guy, sectarian and psycho... "they are worried... about a woman with THAT life story, who might actually be a danger to others or to the child, or who might become homeless!" then Mrs. Brandt from the authorities said... "yes, definitely suspicious, who knows how hard they should crack down and prevent all of this" but the guy grinned and said, "well, she doesn't pose a danger in that sense, but thanks for the tip!" you don't have to be related... to..."

I play with my dick. And then I laugh. And then I tap dance. It's probably the only thing we have left to do. The others run to their temples. They buy food that makes them sick. Food that makes them poor, because of the monster's common sense, if people all discovered that it would be better to keep their own chickens, that would be no gain in the long run.

The society may have been beneficial
but nobody supported the women in everyday life
if they were critical they ended up in prison
they lived like in a big tree that in reality had no roots,
no homeland can be seen on the map people knew the GDR as...
the same picture, experienced also by children and women of "the bunglers"
who went over at the time the wall was built,
for the sake of a career and comfort for the future,
just to cause mischief in the West, the children saw the rule of patriarchs,
like that of Honecker, as oppressive and also....
grey, leveled-out, egalitarian
monotonous, where the women are different struggle for equality
where equality only existed in appearance.

I saw how the background of this damn sick chicken is overpowering, that
she hated me for one main reason or another, because she was getting older
and didn't have a real family yet or feel like she belonged to people, then
saw me in positive, neighborly kindness with my beautiful dog and was
soooo jealous of it, thought the envy belonged to people who had a real life
instead of her. She wasn't young anymore, didn't feel childishly young
anymore, just felt a strong hatred. As if this urge to exorcise that made her
finally give the reason that this chameleon was lying about me, that I was
stalking her, but it was the other way around, in the days and nights she was
putting me down. She now knows that she is SICK and needs real help. That
was at least six attempts by the landlord to calm her down. Then two police
officers were at her door six times in total, so twelve. Then the court made
her pay the police a sum of 1000 euros for her paranoid insults to me, and
the police felt very sorry for me on the phone that I had to put up with that.
Then six letters followed from the landlord's board, including my letter to
them. And finally, that morning, when I had an appointment with my
lawyer, I managed to get hold of this one therapist in the hallway, with
whom I spoke briefly and clearly that this nine-year terrorization had to stop
NOW, otherwise she would hear from me! And at the end, and after more
weeks of terror, this responsibility that lasted a few days longer came about.

She finally understood what she was doing there, there was a witness here a few times, and he said that if she started again from the beginning, he would be a witness again. She had heard his deep male voice early in the morning and then that finally gave her the impetus to stop. In almost all residential areas, the tenants' associations have come to an agreement with the Diakonie that the apartments they rent will allow severely mentally handicapped people to move into completely normal houses, regardless of the outcome. There are scenes all around here. It is simply intolerable. Seems like an act of no thought, not wanting to deal with any consequences from decisions. In hope of no one will dare to complain or claim any rights, legal or human, maybe that cicken above has now chlamydia, then last week dated a Syrian man, or otherwise cries still with 50 that she didn't make her 10th class at school !

The one who is always out of breath, he lacks calm,
the one who is always a checker, he doesn't allow himself any inspiration,
he doesn't let anything come to him, the effort is written all over his face,
he goes at everything at full speed, he lacks dedication,
he shows inferior energy or love, always throws suggestions into his breaks,
he always wants to know what to do, all doors are supposedly open to him,
but he seems presumptuous, he is only concerned with his navel, didn't see it
as a spontaneous idea, I won't believe him, he'd move mountains for me!

Has any woman in Germany ever thought
about agreeing to marry a man like that,
in a way that lacks empathy,
in response to a convoluted proposal
from 10,000 kilometers away?
That's like being reduced to a drinks machine
that has just fallen over, but that only the one person
who comes over an hour later
has permission to pick you up again?
And that's just because he's paid to do it???

218

I'd also like to let you have your say!
When will you decide, as always, dear friend, you have enough to do.
That's the least you can do, Westie USA, to ingratiate with Europeans,
to understand that the term "three quarters to twelve" exists here.
But THEY CAN'T!

But then we're always supposed to be their superglue,
which every US citizen can use for all their purposes.
Is the elite school always a haven of extreme abuse?
In its greed, it demands threefold sponsorship from personalities.
But it covers up the abuse by saying that children actually still
have to be submissive, that according to slaughtering,
they would rather kill others, and conceal the truth
until a child is murdered. Since the Holocaust, everyone still knows
the wording today: "He is not actually a bad person and the fact
that he used young people is only because he was seducing them.
Everything could have been so beautiful if the tyrant had not been here.
This perpetrator was always good to me."
i checked a little in my wording today, this is awesome clear bringing the
Schleswig to the point, because such a perfidious victim of a childs death is
in our moms' eyes a murder, and this will be never be forgotten !
the perfidious trick was in such minds, to just chaise several kids in school
to suicide, for fun, and all see it, but none does anything, until just the one
of them darkskinned with only 10 years old is killed, to warn all above the
poor ones from that day on, that poor people, that alone educating, and
critical and human people on school no more wanted, you see, ONE
DEAD ? you want this for your kids in future ? this was the sudden
foundation of the future new elite school in our town Schleswig and my son
was the one of them who luckily survived.

"For some are in the darkness, And others are in the light
And those in the light are seen Those in the darkness are not seen."

Good morning everyone.

219

We walked without knowing where the road was headed. We trusted people who had no friends or loved ones. We thought we had landed on a safe shore. But they were illusions to forget the days. The philosopher says.

The worst thing about betrayal is that it does not come from an enemy. The betrayal that goes to the heart. That is why the intense pain hollows you out from the inside and would kill you, no longer seeing the greyness around you, no longer hearing the laughter of the world, no longer feeling what is being said, no longer suspecting the tears of others, but the railway line, throwing yourself in front of it... so close!

Life is like the moon. Sometimes you find it full and bright and sometimes empty and dark. A traitor is someone who smiles in your face.

The beginning is for everyone and the continuation is for heroes. We trust in our strength without boasting and we respect the strength of others without fearing it.

Every life consists of new beginnings every day, but we are all trapped, repeating it again and again in different places, while the fruit on the bushes makes you the same tea every day.

The novel always ends with a farewell to the person you fought for. Don't try to understand everything, because too much light blinds you. Most people cannot even see the colors in the light! On the long journey, choose someone whose company you never tire of, because the company is more important than the journey.

In the Arab countries you watch the train, your life and youth disappear before your eyes, and you can't do anything.

It's like... there will always be handsome men even if we walk straight towards them, they look at us with delight, everyone knows the mischief, because they never stay in a woman's life !

I never wanted to enter the SHOW COMPETITION
I didn't think of it, but which friend's arm, please,
would put itself around my shoulder?
But no one who kissed me, announced the engagement to me.
And even less chance, putting his hand down on his stomach in front of
everyone, announces that a miracle is about to be born, in the coming cold
winter, that's no small reward, so if you like playing strip poker with friends,
according to the motto, whoever wins, can put something back on.
Well, now that I'm my age, old fool, no one would have the chance
to FAKE me like that ! HAHAHAHA

Imagine that love is a stranger
whose neck you kiss on the street at night?
Wouldn't that somehow electrify you?
Did it create a memory of rock'n'roll in your morning?
Anyone who enjoys this privilege in life,
that someone likes them because there is a connection,
that they are both chosen as their child,
will perhaps realize that very evening ...
before they go to bed that many people
in their lives have been missing just
that one thing, that one kiss on the neck!
It is not me who undresses for others,
but it is me who makes others naked, then wants to paint them,
and not be the one who makes himself naked for others.
Why does no one want to understand that?
What is it really about, you people?
Is it about the future, that of your children?
or is it about the blurriness in the relationship of love?
have people understood that it would probably now
be a little warmer every day, so much warmer, until people no longer notice,
that they might lose their minds, then have to buy their minced meat
for spaghetti vegan, only without meat?

All businesses will soon go under.
All appliances will break.
Banks will go under.
Children will never come back.
Girls are happy to be rescued,
boys are happy to be rescued girls,
whose parents themselves reject the language,
saved from their mother tongue,
girls want to learn another,
be more perfect than they can master their own words,
be more adept at something,
in a matter that denies their origins,
to look down on themselves, and to say without shame,
that this does not harm them, it is called aging.

Europe is a brilliant place. Europe is old.
Not a haven for fundamentalists.
We don't have to act old. We don't have to look for roots.
We can't find any roots anywhere else either
like in the so-called "West" because they don't exist there !

Music is not made up of tones.
It is the gap between tones. Personality does not exist.
It is just not a new invention.
It is not an irritation of others.
It is not a justification to others.
It is not a request to explain yourself.
Personality is just the sum of what we do individually,
and the connecting line between them,
it is never fixed, it can always change,
it does not exist, it means nothing,
the whole universe does not exist,
so why should something ridiculous
like a "personality" exist?

I learned that coal is black and that
if we wash it repeatedly it will not change.
I learned that imagination depends on....
how far you may have understanding,
how good you have empathy,
how strong you show solidarity,
how clear you speak all out,
how tolerant you bring critics,
how balanced you embrace,
how welcome are the weak to you.
HAPPY BIRTHDAY TO YOU FRIEND !

KEEP IT FLAT!
I dreamed that the people in Schleswig who consider themselves to be the
most distinguished, Viking insiders, long-established, respected, at the
forefront of everything, ... are actually a bunch of young people, the town's
show-offs, who, in the background, are so full of themselves that everyone
has to serve them, and who are lazy, fine people who just spend their time in
their leisure, boringly withdrawn and don't even prepare their own meals
because they have their food brought to them by "meals on wheels".
HAHAHA, in fact, they also take taxis to all the restaurants.....
for "meals on wheels"! Don't make me laugh!!

You enjoy your work.
Only those who do that should leave again.
You approach it diligently and with enthusiasm.
Only for you and the child.
You walk along calmly and calmly, simply greet everyone.
You walk with complete modesty, visibly avoiding the red flags.
You don't walk past friends, and share your humor with them.
You approach everyone with balance,
not seeing anything in black and white.
You go from birthday to evening greeting the fiery sun,
so what's the point of all this, ignoring me?

All young people should shout
"Who's offering us anoraks again, in khaki green with a simple lining?"
everyone will surely enthusiastically throw themselves into the abuse....

All middle-class people shout "Honey, let's swap partners!"
middle age starts with this, when it knows that sex is no longer fun.

All old people should shout,
let's watch the general COMPETITION elegantly and get drunk,
frequently the WASHING MACHINE also stops working!

I have no solution ! Without money should I donate ?
How can someone live forever ? Without wisdom there is no solution.
What is deep sleep ? There is no dental solution.
As they always say with kings, instead of a bite guard,
it is always just the damn bee ! - that is something to think about !

Aren't you fed up with it too?
When the universe is constantly messing things up for you?
When fate is constantly laughing in your face, but not in a nice way?
When obstacles are not only put in your way, but also in your shoe?
Then get ready to change your life from the ground up.
But this time for the better!

As surely as the immigrant looks at the Rhineland,
he says that in the war his country
enjoyed a similar reputation to history, but worse!
As much as the women pass by, they fly over the Rhineland,
all you can see are sausage rolls, and craftsmen,
containers, streets lit up at night, people hanging from the gallows,
and people who are drunk to death,
who you meet every time you look at a house, but worse !

Oh dear, they were supposed to believe
that homemade yogurt was associated with making things yourself!
The Father Stasi Show conveyed that things
were done in a traditional way and that I enjoyed no privileges...
The dirt didn't accumulate - there was nothing in my room.
There was no "private society", not even a name,
because I didn't have a room key.
STANDING OUT from others was almost impossible.
But UP and AWAY was the motto ! Well, don't anyone tell me ÖKO !

Do not ask about the protecting instinct !
Ask the wolve who enters the room. The wolve entering a lighted moment.
Welcome him, but never ask him Who You Are ! Who You like !
Think of nothing ! You are not special !
Unique is the nothing of the universe !
Do you understand the violence took to become this gentle ?
Yes, it is said, that to calm the thought in every moment
and share more often emptiness and love and be prepared
that wonders then appear in a moment when you are aware
that thought might not be needed. Then you need to reflect about.
And better say it out loud.
That's what is LOVE !

- Heike Thieme - Ylva -

You people, you are so good at imagining things...
if there were a war, would you go?
too many deaths of the living, loving, the existing
if there was no work, how was the printer running?
no mood fluctuated, wealth stagnated,
if there was work, and no one went to work?
no longer wanted to feel exploited !
Imagine there is a lot to do, work available, and no one is there,
because politics ignores it!

Nice...isn't it? First they tear the child out of the confinement bed,
almost destroy it in front of their eyes, ends up in pieces in front of me,
so that they can collectively bully me into doing something,
because it was only about ME!!!

I would say, RELAX We ended up in CAR 33 for 27 years
The journey is the destination A FEELING OF LIFE
Looking out a little, I still meditate, Detox, look for a break from work,
34.8% of people like me are no longer given work !
DOESN'T GO WELL – LIKE THE TRAIN But relax about it!

DON'T GET ANGRY, it's not my GAME !
I always wanted to say, you can never fail to please the prince,
first you send an arrow into the middle of his eyes to celebrate,
give him wine, don't even laugh at him,
and explain to him that it's his own birthday,
while the lights around them have all gone out,
.... and no prince thanks you for that !
The bird then has to wave goodbye. He has to live with mum and dad.
He sleeps in mum's bed afterwards,will NEVER hear bells ringing AGAIN !
But his name was Glockner for everyone !!!

THE DISSOCIAL SOCIETY, treat us like that !
They won't recieve a throne for that anymore.
Their own wives run off, and away that people send no comment,
and of course that is well earned !

I hope You enjoy the Day, too, as i am so much delighted now do not have
to check the tax and organize the own house, and bills and things. That i am
still in that age to be able to read my own stoff online. And that i am not the
totally left only one in family.

WE ALL DO KNOW ABOUT THESE TIMES PIRACY that belongs to the
purses of the elderly.

There is enough nonsense. The universe is too little.
God has nothing left. Not everyone is good.
There is hope that not every one of the millions
just thinks they are an a-hole.
But I have nothing to offer except laughter, which spills over
in places even when at rest, then bursting and imploding,
less then as a waterfall because when that happens
then the tears fall with laughter, so the world has no meaning.

NONE ! A direct descendant of the German woman
living nearby is so presumed to be a lesbian
that she completely overlooks her masculine behavior, loud, aloof,
and just like a man, and yet secretly a Christian,
and the proof, in her self-love of a man,
is that she even sleeps with two men,
and when she is in bed with one of them, the man in her joins in.
How, the neighbor thinks... not very understandable,
can someone still cheat on their partner?

See this as proof - that I was always the right mother for Footspring:
when he refused to go to school, when he hated math,
when he was just angry, because the teacher told those kids, that she hated
kids. I let him blow his smoke, then I explained math to him for fun,
he could already write at the age of 3, then I bought philosophy books,
and discussed the world with the child, let him speak,
then he went "Pling!!!!!" and he said, "Now I'm actually enjoying math!"

Other mothers …. tell their sons when they get a 5 in math
"Son, take off your glasses! I'm going to smack you in the face now !"
not explaining to him that it doesn't help, how the world works,
recognizing that his math feeling didn't beat it out of him.

227

The breathtaking, beautiful local women, as the best of all,
always like to distance themselves,
they have such a dream of SOUTH AMERICA!!!!
There they picked out a DOG from the DESERT
and put him on a plane here, demonstrating to EVERYONE
how unique they are because of that, that's why they have a tattoo
on their breastbone of growing jungle vines,
plus a unique, unique, aloof look that makes me LAUGH so much
that I lose my PANTS... and you meet them right there
a second time, and then NEVER AGAIN!!!!!
FOR TEACHERS; who already see THINKING as an ILLNESS!
Politics wants to provide a solution.... little fat boys become soldiers,
pubescently telling children that weapons open doors for them,
the morbid, chubby pseudo-idea of the Waldorf children creating an Indian
life for themselves, promising that their dancing children will fix it,
the bald-headed 60's today on the right, the stoned teachers' children today
on the left, the teachers on the fringes of everything happening,
saying goodbye to cruelty from kindergarten onwards,
always against individuals, the weaker ones,
"The less we see, ... the less will happen!"

Don't read me if my words that put out a forest fire can't put out the fire in
your heart.

Don't read me if my words that aflame an extinguished fire into flame don't
create a spark in you.

Don't read me if my words that revive a dry, cracked soil don't awaken a
sprout in your soul.

Do you know what it's like to be a brilliant, handsome guy? He's superficial,
manipulated by looks, and is power hungry. He abuses for love, drops them
all like hot potatoes, no end, even when people almost die in the process.
He's gone, just gone, rivers of tears, fears,and flowing blood behind his loss.

And a beautiful person just came and went, the way they do, just because they can. Coming and going. He almost asks for money to get fucked, such is his self-love. He promises anyone what he wants to hear, his wants and needs are simple, right above his wide eyes that can be seen on the front. He touches you and then the stupid fall you are part of. A CHAMELEON in the love atmosphere. I'm not stupid to fall for this, promise! Before that I would have fallen in love with a beauty beast, my Mable would enter my room and actually give me the fuck finger like she really did once, hehe. That was the first real shock of his life. It's funny to see a protective Labrador of your heart come in while your dog stumbles in his little collar and that paw gets caught in it and holds it tighter and tighter to me while the second other one tries to fool me. He said he was apparently with the wolf and the wolf asked who he was, he just told the wolf "I am a friend of the lion" trying to fool me. But little did he know that at that very moment I was meditating and feeling like a wolf with an enlightening awareness of peace in mind and light in head when my dog came into the room with his little problem. So I immediately responded to the foolish attempt: "And the wolf was aware of an enlightening moment when the dog entered in the person of my own mother!" I told him, and this prompt response in the other direction destroyed his desire to disparage my wolf.

That was checkmate again and again.

Good night and sleep well friends ! And I promise you I will go to bed in my own skin and not pretend to be anyone else when I get up in the morning or tell myself the lie that I would be a new and better person just because I woke up!

haha that was Good One, if i sometimes research the night dream thought of me, i am totally agreeing. We do not have to force our changings, they appear in few hours every day.

Raise your head, your enemies are watching you, my friend.

...Time heals everything... But !...Half the statement is true and the other half is false Time doesn't heal everything..! It's just that...with time you learn how to bear the pain.

The plain truth is that the planet does not need more successful people. But it desperately needs more peacemakers. There were days when I wished someone would support me, even if it was just out of courtesy. These are the same days that taught me to stand tall on my own.

Nothing is worth turning your favorite things into harsh lessons !
Nobody calls one Child helpless.
No family calls one person abandoned.
No hater calls one good person to be evil.
The Number Eleven will teach this You all !

The keys to hearts have no other copies...
If you lose it, know it will stay locked.
Forever in your face. .. I am the one who gets up after every fall and gets up as if it were... I challenge life, circumstances and despair.

I am that one caring for my emotion.
I am that one treating my garden well.
I am not in the least afraid of defending myself,
especially against very stupid and unfriendly people.
Those who cowardly intimidate others are also those who do not have the friendliness of the neighborhood, who have not learned to refrain from threatening individual passers-by.

That, dear people, is what fat, old, stupid bastards do!
INTIMIDATE, UNFRIENDLINESS, THREATEN

The family always has someone sitting on the toilet.
It has to be someone. It wasn't me who fell over on stage with one arm.
A holiday home on the island has vanished. It is not her will.

To invite a mother like me and her child.
A family celebration that doesn't happen.
First an aunt would fall from the clouds.
Meet a sister in shame for her high spirits.
Nobody wants to meet her seriously.
THE FAMILY at THEIR CELEBRATION! Just take it.

I believe that prostitution only exists,
as a blueprint, so to speak, because there are fat aunts,
with pearls around their necks, a choleric in tow,
who bully subordinates,
who demand the highest level of sex via advertisement,
who were late,
who bite every trainee on the nose,
who demand subordination,
who fire people as quickly as possible,
who serve on behalf of romance,
who make good money from it,
who have others make themselves beautiful,
and who always offer their poodles water.

Everyone wants to be a virgin. All old people want to stay young.
All fear frigid tendencies. All want everything for free.
All shy away from youth. All think laziness is unromantic.
All only do it for themselves. All fear their own decadence.
All think the statements of competent people are competition.

The woman stands in front of the gigolo, he says it's normal,
it's the first time, we're both standing here and we're nervous,
we both don't know if it's going to work,
we'll always call her "first customer"
and everyone will be a "pretty woman", hehe
as far as today's businesswoman is concerned,
he sees it as totally spontaneous and relaxed.

When you see that some people laugh at your loss, know that you have made them cry many times. The increase in a person's status lies in his realism, in knowing his limits and in recognizing where he is and when he is... Throwing the hook into a sea with rough waves, that is trust. Waiting a long time to get something, that is patience. And when you don't get anything, that is satisfaction, says the philosopher. Life did not require us to be strong, it forced us to do so. Knowing the truth is still the most difficult thing in this life. A conversation with a wise man is better than 10 years of studying books !

Everyone will betray you... even the woman you gave everything to, the woman you fought to make a wonderful life for will suddenly turn you into a huge graveyard and turn her back on you, the woman you were afraid to scratch will tear you apart terribly without any mercy.
I know the woman betraying me.
I know the woman denying me.
I know the woman stealing from me.
I know the woman scratching me.
I know the woman turn back on me.
I know the paranoid woman fighting me.
But i was never afraid of those. They are all sick people.

Inside us, ancient cities whose inhabitants have departed, leaving behind images and lasting memories. They took our souls, our voices and our laughter and emigrated. They left the windows of waiting wide open. They left silence in our city... and sadness within us uproots our souls..!

I know such cowards, too. Hiding their truth of life, denying their moms, searching heros to be, and see them falling behind,
then come crawling back, those who find the child inside
finally then twenty five years later, and still find themselves heroes,
then leave their truest friend behind, and advertize their proud bravety.
Pretend you trust people, but you don't. All birds have a home to sleep in, except for birds that practice freedom. They die outside their home.

And when you wake up, you find that your mind is laughing, your heart is crying and your soul is lost...! Something hurts me that I don't know.. and maybe I know it but I love it. Be kind to me, life.

In the dark went a couple in front of me, i guessed if two men, or one woman, when she shreaked out loud, and i knew a lovers pair, her guy made a joke. Then when i passed on them joking that we are harmless, and they said that lovers are harmless, too, usually, as good as it gets every day better. Then i said, that way i am not ticking, like a sticky conservative his daily motto to become a better person every single day. But that i am aware and let those people believe that i am trusting them all, but i don't. As well as i know as mature being, the others i don't trust, that i did not have to be a better one for those.

This is surely the great illusion of trust, just because you say it is so you say it is safe. Haha never like that, it is a saying of the redflags, all in all liars, cowards and hypocrites, while they say trust you, keep your fist in your pocket and count if the money is still there, no first the money is safe, they all know that passersby would kill them if they knew there was any in the pants, funny image, those rich mates and females, with loss in the pants, but in the fist in the pocket worthy dollars. Compensating, ahh the lesser the sex the bigger the purse. More fun playing with one's sex, though.

The money won't react the same way. Just childish fun, ahh you never know, if people have enough of money, they could feed all hundred kicks, and triggers, and fetish, but sounds a little bit sick, to feed the kicks and triggers with money, as if people were an autmatic machinell sex triggering robot. Some almost are, but you know that already. Kicks and triggers fed grows more fat and greedy, almost all psychic troubles make them fat, that i still wonder how the youngsters grow like that fat. I see the tendency to education, the lesser teachers, the rotten schools, the bad equipment, the drugs on the playground, the legalized drug, the fuck shitty smartphone, the lesser ability to concentrate, the parents ignoring the kids future skills to teach, the parents who leave all education to some few pedagoges.

The lesser discipline to follow the lesson, the lesser respect, and irritation from all directions, the noise in school, the bully, the competition to be better, all this lets them grow greedy and wanting all more and more, and work for not a single day. If that continues, the worthy thought of non violence gets loss, the consciousness to stop before harming, the lesser solidarity among people, the Conscience to all evil will dissapear.

What ever, as well as kids now better not being born, sameway those mature beings are better told not to be confronted to the kids of today. Time to rest and relax a bit, i see poor people all days on the street, and sick people standing at every corner, mindless elderly wagging along on the road, and cruel fierce neighbors who have the privilege to work, the fighter dogs in the leash of sick addicted.

Time to rest and relax a bit, i see poor people all days on the street, and sick people standing at every corner, mindless elderly wagging along on the road, and cruel fierce neighbors who have the privilege to work, the fighter dogs in the leash of sick addicted.

In order to find the right path, you must first get lost.....When lions become friendlier, hyenas become bolder....Fight for your dreams and your dreams will fight for you ...Nowadays they breed dogs in shelters and children on the streets...There will come a day when you realize that turning a page is the best feeling in the world, because you will realize that there is much more to the book than that page you were stuck on..!

I wanted to tell you that everyone has disappointed me and that I am afraid of everyone but you, but you abandoned me before I told you. We loved life and wanted to live the way we wanted. She cheated on us and forced me to live the way she wanted. When I was a young brat, cast away by her, to multiply among others who lived on the streets, I wore a hat, and the skirt and the sweater that I knitted with my fingers, and read in books about everything, often gave away the best books, how I was "GONE AWAY" as a young woman, as a child even on the street.

I will, I promised you, never bow my head in front of people who declare themselves to be my enemy because I feel like they are watching me. Yes, that sounds good, in many ways, as I expected. But I wonder how you deal with emigrating and having a little mom with a child? But since people have the right ideas early on, I'm quite sure of that, I'll grant you that, people. It's also nice that another mom who is alone has a different experience than me.

Single mothers are stuck in society, helpless anyway, and it's not a nice feeling, as if the bureaucracy and all the workforce wanted to teach women their "lesson" on each and every one of them, so that they would still end up humiliated and without a job. Thirdly, they bully you as if they wanted to break your will, then see you collapse with guilt and call it a "conversion", as if they were putting their own personal stamp on you for everyone's fun, deceit and hypocrisy, just to distract themselves from their malaise and have something to laugh about!

I wanted to tell you that everyone has let me down and that I'm afraid of everyone except you, but you abandoned me before I told you. We loved life and wanted to live the way we wanted. She cheated on us and forced me to live the way she wanted. The bitch who called herself our mother.

The little girls,
the first ones the son brings home,
in the anal phase, i.e. eating,
in the naive phase, i.e. grief,
in the longing for the prince,
so off to the theater with them,
in the greed for recognition,
so let them make statements,
no matter how wrong they are,
otherwise they get a slap on the wrist,
because then there will only be schnitzel.

I didn't stand in front of the guys like a complete idiot.

Only today do I remember them how it was at school.
No one even had to have died, how easy it was to contact me ?
It was never mentioned, because they thought I was the prettiest in the class.
Anyway, 60 years have already passed, what am I supposed to think of such
sudden interest, such requests for solidarity? One of them called me his
sister, because his second wife had a life like mine, and said that I hope we
have nice days together in the years to come !

I know that a child always signals to you the immense love you have for
being good to them and looking after them. My child was also born on the
Kiel beach, but he was snatched from me in all his brutality. Until today I
could never have imagined how I would have spent happy hours with my
little son on the Kiel beach. It was probably too long ago. Just as my son
swore to me that he no longer has the slightest good thing to say about any
other Schleswiger, apart from his mother. So I assume that I will never make
friends with people from the Kiel scene again after they denounced me
there.

Good, then I'm happy. I always thought that once a friend from afar gets a
taste of Sweden, he'll be off the farm for the next few years. It's easier to
endure it, knowing that this isn't the case.
Take a mother's newborn and mistreat both,
then rob her of motherhood, and portray her as STUPID,
stupid enough to be at the mercy of the powers that be,
and deny her intelligence, declare her guilty,
incapable, unsuitable for work or motherhood,
steal her peace, monitor her gait, and call it socially simply denying
a super intelligent woman the so-called "intelligent gene"
in order to torture her to the utmost ! TEST - When will she break out ??

Having a choice in the country is a bit like... the mother forward,
who cleans everyone's pipes, who kicks the military,
who throws everything at a friend, who sends a daughter forward,
who is even dumber than her mother, who sees insults as classic,

Voyeurs throw food then away, who only sees the word "AWESOME"
in a positive sense of "FUCKING GOOD"
where there is a small photo hanging on the wall.

HIGH FIVE! ... such mothers run off spreading false talk
in the neighborhood, spreading out as if they were part of the clientele,
as they have already been told, helping out children...
"People who absolutely need it, really need it, joining those
who need a little more attention for themselves!" ...
who thinks their child is someone like that,
embarrassingly outs him or her, making "their child" horribly ridiculous.
Look at the Germans ! They are "friends of Putin" again
because WE GIVE and the RUSSIANS TAKE
that means in concrete terms PUTIN wants to RAP all German women
across the board in order to consolidate political power
and the East Germans are happy to let it happen !

Politics today, contemporary, coolly put, weak tones for thin content
fashionable confusion election today and not asked tomorrow
pop-up parties without constants, one is put up and sings the other's songs
the "LIGA of liberal liberals" or "Lol" for short, party for "the footballers",
the party with the "shining figure of social thought", the "kitten" party
one wants to represent "the song" in a partisan way,
as an ego-techno-lawyer-doctors song, one wants "the rhythm"
as a clerical message rhythm dance, one wants "the tax message"
as a bureaucratic cubist corpse, the "three" from the very top,
who rule for "three" years next to them,
the "kings" of the unsuccessful.

Society must keep the finances flat ! Today you need Moncy !
Teach your kids swimming, less water, high cost,
bathing in french ideal mineral water, no more pool noodles,
kids game with dolphin in the basin and Athlete's foot the status symbol !

She wastes her life in idleness. She is partly a furniture.
She has to be proud to a highness. She obeys HIS love.
She believes in hollow compliment.
She leaves and gives place to another slave.
She messes with no man anymore.

As in countries, completely systematic: every village idiot involved
the teenager, the holy virgin, the up-and-coming girl, in podcast, influencer,
the village beauties. Mafia organization - just go to the disco !
sexual harassment - just go to work !
Violation of of human rights - just marry a man

820-1 DIN NORM

You have it, you can do it, what you have,
because you can of the working class compared to the stigmatized
population

1. Everything has to be a lie, - feigned interest - alleged allergies - lost
presumption of innocence - contemptuous assessment of people - reduced
willingness to work - feigned victimhood - feigned birthday date - colossal
political no-go statement - attempt to make enemies instead of friends

2. Injuring someone in an ambush
3. Embarrassing someone in an obvious attack
4. Throwing stones at other people's children to celebrate
5. Praising the colonial era without inhibition
6. Staying with your parents
7. Swimming, even if only in a beach bikini, but not unchlorinated
8. Showing off disabled family members
9. Separation from the normal neighborhood
10. Brutal expression, intimidation by aggressive dogs
11. Young, against the church, everything in a commanding tone
12. overestimation of one's own abilities

« When composing the working committees,
the principle must be taken into account that the interested parties are
represented an appropriate proportion to one another ! »

SL-H...10.09.2024, HEIKE THIEME – YLVA
LET'S GET TO THE POINT !
What would Lord of the Rings have been like if single parents... turned old
into young, stuck to every place, felt rejected at every job, raised their arms
at every come-on, breasts out at every red flag, opened their eyes at every
marriage ad, spread their legs at every gift of bread, downloaded the app at
every sex straw, went to the cinema at every children's film, celebrated at
every sausage, bared their teeth at every visit to the dentist, spoke of panic
at every white face, hoped for membership at every invitation, made a show
out of every Whatsapp peep?

THINK LULL !
Last person without a podcast !
No app wanted in 2011.
My first smartphone in 2021
at the age of almost 60.
Sorry, anyone who is raising children,
who wants to work,
who has responsibility,
who has ideas,
who has never needed therapeutic help,
is also strongly advised against it !

I HAVE SEEN CORPSES !
Doctor in a coat, he can shake, your word to Redmann,
you are a soulful man, look up and believe,
are not a machine, take it up and be lye, that steals your time,
he sits through the hours, plays Monopoly on the beach,
of course smells of the Maldives, the divas lie by the swimming pool,
swimming noodles are child's play, French mineral water in the break room,

THE OATH OF HIPPOCRATES, he swears by the TOTAL TRUTH
the DOCTOR today doesn't need an apple,
the apple a DAY saves you the doctor, so people, leave the DOCTORS
and swear by your own knowledge, you ALL have it !
START THINKING !
Blonde girls are not from Bond.
They fell from the Sky.
Piglets from the factory.
Daddy's rich girl.
Just there, all alone.
Sees into other people's lives.
Just a bit of a loser, single last year.
Likes sporty women.
She's a smart choice for deluxe.
The rest of the world can go to hell.
Wants you as a prince, right there.
Penetrate away from the counter.
Because she's sexually breathtaking.
Stands at the meat market just for you.
She only eats vegan, I promise.
She knows so many followers, it's hard work.
She needs to recover in his arms.
The price is hot, if you don't grab it now!
In her eyes, you've already lost!